THE ULTIMATE
BREAD MACHINE
COOKBOOK
FOR BEGINNERS

*Easy-to-Follow Recipes for a Perfect
Loaf Every Time. Step-By-Step Baking
Guide with Simple, Healthy, Whole
Grain, and Gluten-Free Options*

STEWART BROOKS

TABLE OF CONTENTS

INTRODUCTION

Welcome to the "Bread Machine Cookbook for Beginners," your trusty baking companion! Using a bread maker brings back nostalgic memories and comforting scents. The aroma of freshly baked bread in a cozy kitchen is beloved by many, evoking warmth and familiarity.

The smell of baking bread is more than just a sensory experience; it transports us to our memories and breaks down barriers between the present and the past. It transports us back to our childhood kitchen days when we watched in awe as kneaded dough underwent a miraculous change while baking.

It raises the question, "What is the driving force behind this profound emotional response to the aroma of baking bread?" The answer lies deep inside human psychology, specifically in how our brains interpret smells. This link enables smells to evoke strong emotional memories, often even before we know the perfume. Therefore, the scent of baked bread can transport us back to fond memories of the past by evoking sentiments of warmth, comfort, and home.

Baking bread in a bread maker has a greater meaning than just the smell and the act of baking. Indeed, it is a representation of affection and care. Bread is associated with nourishment, family, community and is a staple food in almost every culture on the planet.

In today's hectic environment, the convenience of store-bought bread may eventually supplant the time-honored practice of baking bread at home. However, the taste and delight of a freshly baked homemade bread loaf cannot be matched by any commercially produced loaf. In addition, nothing compares to the distinct scent that fills the house during baking and adds to the cozy ambiance.

Filling your home with the aroma of warm, freshly baked bread, is the key point of our trip through this book. We work hard to replace store-bought fake bread full of preservatives with healthier, tastier, and incredibly delicious homemade bread.

We want to invite you to join us on this exciting bread-making journey and bring the smell of freshly baked bread into our homes once more. Our mission extends beyond simple baking to include making heartfelt memories, practicing patience and mindfulness.
Let's get started on this adventure.

WHAT IS A BREAD MACHINE?

THE HISTORY OF THE BREAD MACHINE'S CREATION

A bread machine is an automated kitchen appliance designed for baking bread. It consists of a heating chamber and a mixing mechanism, which together allow for the automatic mixing of ingredients, rising of the dough, and baking of the bread without user intervention after the process has begun.

The history of bread machines began in Japan, where in 1986, the company Matsushita Electric (now Panasonic) released the first bread machine for home use. This device was developed by a team of engineers led by Ikuya Tamizawa, who aimed to create a device capable of automatically mixing dough and baking bread to simplify the bread baking process at home. Their invention used a unique dough kneading method that mimicked the hand movements of a baker, thus solving the problem of uneven kneading, which was characteristic of early attempts at automating the process.

After its introduction to the Japanese market, bread machines quickly gained popularity and began to spread to other countries, including the United States and Europe, in the late 1980s and early 1990s. Consumers liked these devices for their ability to simplify the bread baking process, making it more accessible and convenient for people without previous baking experience.

With technological advancements, modern bread machines have become much more functional than their predecessors. They are equipped with various baking programs for different types of bread, including gluten-free bread, French bread, whole grain bread, and many others. Additionally, modern models offer various crust control settings and delay start timers, allowing users to customize the baking process according to their needs. Bread machines have also become more energyefficient and user-friendly, with many models now featuring touch control panels and LCD displays for user convenience. Furthermore, some of the latest models include removable baking pans, making cleaning easier and offering the possibility of preparing more than just a bread.

THE ADVANTAGES OF USING A BREAD MACHINE OVER TRADITIONAL BREAD BAKING METHODS

Bread machines offer several advantages over the traditional manual method of bread baking, making the process more convenient, less time-consuming, and the results consistently high-quality. Here are a few key advantages of using a bread machine:

- **Convenience:**

A bread machine auto-mates the entire bread baking process, from dough mixing and rising to baking. You simply need to add the ingredients, select the appropriate program, and wait for the process to complete.

- **Time-saving:**

Baking bread manually requires active observation and participation at every stage. With a bread machine, you can engage in other activities while your bread is being prepared.

- **Less mess:**

Traditional bread baking requires the use of numerous utensils and tools, which then need to be cleaned. A bread machine limits the entire process to one pan, which is easily cleaned after use.

- **Consistency of results:**

A bread machine ensures a consistent quality level every time, thanks to precise temperature and baking time control. This removes the worry about overly hard or insufficiently risen bread.

- **Variety:**

Modern bread machines offer various baking programs for different types of bread, including gluten-free options, and the ability to experiment with ingredients and additives.

- **Delay timer functions:**

Most models are equipped with delay start timers, allowing users to adjust the baking process so that freshly baked bread is ready exactly

BREAD MACHINES MAY VARY:

- **Bread machines** by its size:

From compact models that easily fit on a small kitchen countertop to larger appliances designed for baking a large amount of bread. The choice depends on the space you're willing to allocate for the device and the amount of bread you plan to bake regularly. Larger models may even have two baking pans, speeding up the bread preparation process and allowing you to bake twice as much at once.

- **By the size of the finished loaf:**

Some models offer the ability to bake loaves of different sizes – from small, perfect for one or two people, to large, satisfying the needs of an entire family. It's important to

choose a model with the options you need to fully meet your baking needs.

- **By the presence of a viewing window:**

Some bread machines are equipped with a viewing window, which allows you to observe the baking process without the need to open the lid of the device. This can be particularly useful for those who like to control the baking process and make adjustments to recipes on the fly.

- **By additional features:**

Modern bread machines may have a wide range of additional functions, including settings for baking gluten-free bread, programs for making jams and yogurt, as well as options for baking various types of dough, such as French bread, whole grain bread, etc. The choice of a model with a certain set of functions depends on your preferences and how you plan to use the device.

SETTINGS AND ADJUSTMENTS IN BREAD MACHINES

Before baking bread in a bread machine, users can adjust several parameters to tailor the baking process to a specific recipe or personal preference. Here's a detailed overview of the key parameters and settings:

- **Baking Programs**

Depending on the model, bread machines offer a variety of programs for different types of bread and gluten-free,

gluten-free, quick bake, dough, jam, etc. Each program automatically adjusts the kneading, rising, and baking times for optimal results.

- **Loaf Size**

Many bread machines allow you to select the size of the loaf you plan to bake. This can range from small (about 500 g, 1 pound) to medium (about 750 g, 1 1/2 pounds)

6

and large (1 kg or more, 2 pounds). The size selection impacts the quantity of ingredients and the duration of the baking program.

- **Crust Color**

Users can adjust the crust color to their liking, choosing between light, medium, or dark. This changes the duration of the last baking phase, affecting the color and crispness of the crust.

- **Delay Timer**

This feature allows you to set a delayed start for the baking process, so the bread is ready exactly when it's convenient for you. For example, you can load the ingredients in the evening and set the bread machine so that fresh bread is ready by breakfast.

- **Temperature Settings**

Some models allow adjusting the baking temperature for specific recipes or types of dough, providing even greater control over the baking process.

- **Pause/Stop**

This function lets users stop the machine at any stage of baking to add ingredients that shouldn't be mixed from the beginning (e.g., nuts or raisins) or simply to check the dough's condition.

- **Custom Programming**

Some advanced bread machine models offer the ability to create custom baking programs, where you can set the duration of each process stage (kneading, rising, baking) individually. This is ideal for experienced users who want to experiment with unconventional recipes or special types of dough.

- **Automatic Dispenser for Additional Ingredients**

Some bread machines are equipped with automatic dispensers for additional ingredients, such as seeds, nuts, and raisins. These dispensers automatically add ingredients at the right moment in the process, ensuring their even distribution throughout the dough.

- **Signals**

Many bread machines emit auditory signals that mark important stages in the baking process, such as the end of kneading or the time to add ingredients that shouldn't be mixed from the beginning.

- **Removable Baking Pan**

Almost all modern bread machines come with removable baking pans, making it easier to remove the finished bread and clean the pan. Many of them are coated with non-stick material for additional convenience.

These parameters and settings allow bread machine users to fully adapt the baking process to their needs and preferences, opening up unlimited possibilities for experimenting with the baking of various types of bread and other products.

POPULAR PROGRAMS IN BREAD MACHINES

Most modern bread machines are equipped with baking programs that not only make the bread-making process easier but also more flexible. Here are some of the most popular programs you might find in a bread machine:

- **Basic/Normal**

This mode is designed for baking standard white or wheat breads with a medium baking time. It's perfectly suited for most traditional bread recipes.

- **Whole Grain**

A special mode for breads using whole grain or coarse flour. This mode provides a longer rising time for the dough to accommodate the heavier flour structure.

- **French**

For baking breads with a crispy crust and a light, airy interior, like traditional French bread. This mode ensures longer baking and shorter rising times.

- **Quick**

This mode significantly reduces baking time, making it ideal for quickly preparing bread. However, bread baked in quick mode may have a less traditional texture and aroma.

- **Gluten-Free**

Specially developed for baking bread without using gluten. This mode takes into account the peculiarities of gluten-free ingredients, ensuring optimal conditions for rising and baking.

- **Bake**

A mode used for the maturation of dough and baking without the mixing phase. This is perfect for dough that was kneaded by hand or prepared in advance.

- **Dough**

This mode is intended for mixing and rising dough without further baking. It's perfect for preparing dough for pizza, buns, or other products that you want to shape and bake separately.

- **Jam/Preserves**

Some bread machines have a special mode for making jams and preserves. This allows using the bread machine not only for baking bread but also for creating homemade canned fruits and berries.

- **Cinnamon/Sweet Baking**

This special setting is for baking breads with sweet ingredients, such as cinnamon or candied fruit, which require a special baking mode to prevent burning.

- **Bake Only**

This mode is used when you only need to bake, not knead the dough. It's ideally suited for those instances when you already have prepared dough and just want to use the bread machine for baking.

COOKING CYCLES IN
BREAD MACHINES

Bread machines utilize several standard cooking cycles. Here's an overview of the main cycles:

DOUGH KNEADING CYCLE

- **Purpose:** Mixing ingredients and kneading dough.
- **Action:** The bread machine mixes dry ingredients and liquid to form a uniform dough.
- **Time:** Typically takes from 15 to 20 minutes.
- **Usage:** The foundation for all types of bread and dough.

FIRST RISING CYCLE

- **Purpose:** Allow the dough to rise, developing texture and volume.
- **Action:** The dough remains in a warm chamber, where fermentation occurs and volume increases.
- **Time:** Usually lasts from 45 minutes to 1 hour.
- **Usage:** Essential for all types of bread to develop texture and aroma.

PUNCH DOWN CYCLE

- **Purpose:** Decrease the volume of the dough before the second rise.
- **Action:** The bread machine briefly kneads the dough, removing air bubbles.
- **Time:** This stage lasts only a few minutes.
- **Usage:** Prepares the dough for the final rise, improving structure.

SECOND RISING CYCLE

- **Purpose:** The final rise of the dough before baking.
- **Action:** The dough remains warm for rising, ensuring the final volume and shape of the loaf.
- **Time:** Can last from 20 minutes to 1 hour, depending on the recipe.
- **Usage:** Forms the final structure and volume of the bread.

COOLING CYCLE

- **Purpose:** Gradually cool the bread after baking to prevent moisture condensation inside the loaf.
- **Action:** The bread remains in the bread machine with the heating turned off, allowing it to cool slowly.
- **Time:** Not all models have an automatic cooling cycle, but when it is present, it can last from 10 to 30 minutes.
- **Usage:** Prevents the bread from becoming soggy inside, keeping the crumb dry and airy.

Each of these cycles is designed for specific purposes and types of preparation, allowing users to fully utilize the capabilities of their bread machine. It's important to note that the exact duration of each cycle may vary depending on the manufacturer.

Let's take a closer look at the most important cycle - **the bread baking cycle**

THE BREAD BAKING CYCLE

The bread baking cycle in a bread machine is the culmination of the bread-making process, where all the previous stages of dough kneading and rising are completed, and it's time to transform it into finished bread with an appetizing crust and crumb. Here are the details of using this cycle:

- **When it's used:**

The baking cycle automatically starts after the dough rising stages are completed, when the dough has reached the necessary volume and is ready for baking. It's used in all bread-making programs, regardless of the type of bread you are making.

- **How the process occurs:**

During the baking cycle, the bread machine heats up to the optimal temperature for baking the selected type of bread. The temperature and baking time are carefully controlled to ensure even baking and the formation of a characteristic crust. During the baking process, the water contained in the dough turns into steam, which contributes to a light, airy texture of the crumb, while a crust forms on the outside.

- **The purpose of this cycle:**

The baking cycle is necessary for the final transformation of the prepared and risen dough into bread. It ensures not only the baking of the dough to readiness but also the formation of an appetizing crust, giving the bread a finished appearance and desired texture. Additionally, baking activates chemical reactions that contribute to the formation of the bread's aroma and flavor.

- **How long does this cycle typically take:**

The duration of the baking cycle can vary from 30 minutes to 1 hour, depending on the program and the type of bread you are baking. For example, lighter, white breads may bake faster, while denser, whole grain, or gluten-free breads may require more time for baking. On modern bread machines, users can select or adjust the duration of the baking cycle according to the manufacturer and model of their device

THE BREAD MAKING PROCESS

KEY TIPS FOR BREAD MAKING

Making bread in a bread machine may seem like a simple task, but to achieve the perfect result, it's important to follow some key rules. Here's what you need to know:

- **Choose the Right Program:**

Each type of bread requires a specific cooking program optimized for its ingredients and baking technology. For example, whole grain bread needs a longer rising time, while bread made with quick-rise yeast fits a faster program. It's crucial to carefully select the program that matches the recipe and the desired type of bread. To avoid mistakes, choose the program specified in the recipe.

- **Select the Right Temperature Setting:**

Although most bread machines automatically adjust the temperature based on the selected program, some models allow users to adjust the baking temperature. This can be useful for experimenting with new recipes or adjusting the baking process to achieve better texture or crust.

- **Add Ingredients in the Correct Order:**

The correct sequence of adding ingredients is critically important. Typically, water is the first ingredient, followed by sugar, salt, etc. Place the yeast in a small well in the flour so it doesn't come into contact with the liquid and salt. For heavy dough made with whole grains, it's recommended to first add dry ingredients **(flour) and then liquids (water, milk).**

- **Use Scales and Measuring Cups:**

Accuracy in measurements is key to success in bread making. Even small deviations in the quantity of ingredients can significantly impact the result. Use kitchen scales to measure dry ingredients and measuring cups or pitchers for l/iquids to ensure maximum accuracy.

- **Avoid Opening the Lid During Baking:**

Opening the lid of the bread machine during the baking cycle can lead to heat and steam loss, necessary for even baking and crust formation. If you must check the bread's condition, do so quickly and carefully.

- **Checking Bread Readiness:**

If you're unsure whether the bread has baked thoroughly, insert a wooden skewer into the bread's full length after the baking stage. If the skewer comes out wet or with dough residue, the bread needs to bake for some more time.

- **Storing Bread:**

Bread baked in a bread machine doesn't contain preservatives like commercially available bread, so its shelf life is shorter. Store the bread in a cool, dry place and wrap it in storage paper or a clean cloth to keep it fresh longer.

- **Experiment with Ingredients:**

A bread machine allows you to experiment with various types of flour, additives, and flavorings. Don't be afraid to try new combinations, such as whole grain flour, seeds, nuts, dried fruits, or aromatic herbs, to create unique types of bread.

By following these tips and recommendations, you can fully utilize your bread machine's capabilities and enjoy fresh, aromatic bread at home every day.

BASIC INGREDIENTS FOR BREAD MAKING

Making bread in a bread machine requires using basic ingredients, as well as the possibility of including additional ones for variety in flavor and texture. Here are the main ingredients and some tips on their use:

- **Flour -** This is the foundation of any bread. You can use white wheat flour, whole grain, rye, or special blends for gluten-free bread. It's important to use flour of the correct grind – bread machines work well with medium or fine grind flour.

TIP: For better texture and nutrition, try mixing different types of flour, but remember that whole grain flour absorbs more liquid.

- **Water or Other Liquids -** Water is necessary to activate the yeast and form the dough. Milk, buttermilk, or plant-based milk can also be used to add flavor.

TIP: The liquid should be at room temperature or slightly warm, but not hot, to avoid killing the yeast.

- **Yeast -** Active dry yeast or instant (quick-rise) yeast is typically used. They are responsible for raising the dough.

TIP: Add yeast last, after all other dry ingredients, to prevent it from activating prematurely.

- **Salt -** Improves the taste of bread and controls yeast growth, ensuring an even rise.

TIP: Do not let the salt come into direct contact with the yeast, as this can reduce its activity.

- **Sugar or Other Sweeteners -** Sugar nourishes the yeast and helps the dough rise better, adding flavor. Honey, syrups, or alternative sweeteners can also be used.

TIP: Adjust the amount of sugar according to your taste preferences and chosen recipe. Remember, too much sugar can slow down yeast growth.

- **Fats -** Improves the taste of bread and controls yeast growth, ensuring an even rise.

TIP: Fats add softness to the bread and can help keep it fresh longer. Use high-quality fats for a better flavor.

- **Enhancers and Additives -** Dry milk, eggs, seeds (sunflower, sesame, flax), nuts, dried fruits, and herbs can be added for flavor and texture variety.

TIP: Add these ingredients according to the recipe's recommendations or at your discretion, but remember to balance flavors and textures. Add large pieces of nuts or dried fruits during the bread machine's signal to prevent them from being crushed during the initial kneading phase.

GENERAL TIPS FOR USING INGREDIENTS:

- **Always check the freshness of ingredients:** This is especially true for yeast, a key element in dough rise. The freshness of other ingredients will also affect the taste and quality of the bread.
- **Use room temperature ingredients:** Especially for liquids and fats. Room temperature ingredients help the yeast activate evenly and promote better dough rise.
- **Follow recipes and proportions:** While experimenting with ingredients is possible and even encouraged, beginners are advised to follow a tested recipe to ensure success.
- **Adapt recipes to your bread machine:** Depending on the features of your model, you might need to adjust the quantity of ingredients or the duration of cycles. Observe the cooking process and make necessary adjustments.

By following these tips and recommendations, you'll be able to fully utilize the capabilities of your bread machine and enjoy fresh, aromatic bread at home every day.

COMMON PROBLEMS AND SOLUTIONS

These tips will help avoid common mistakes when baking bread in a bread machine and achieve the desired result, regardless of the recipe or type of bread machine used.

#	Problem Name	Cause	Solution
1	**Smoke or steam emitting from the vent during baking**	This can happen if ingredients land on the heating elements or are placed too close to them, or due to oil presence on the heating elements after their first use.	Disconnect the appliance from the power source, let it cool down, and clean the heating elements.
2	**Difficulty removing bread from the pan**	Material particles stuck to the pan.	Soak the pan with the bread in warm water for some time after baking.
3	**Problems with mixing and baking ingredients**	The wrong program selected.	Use a different program.
		The lid was opened several times during baking, affecting the quality of the crust.	Refrain from opening the lid towards the end of baking.
		Incorrect ratio of ingredients.	Check the mixing mechanism and the quantity of ingredients according to the recipe.
4	**Dough does not mix, though motor is running**	Incorrect placement of the pan or too much dough.	Ensure the pan is installed correctly; check the amount of ingredients.
5	**Insufficient bread size or rise**	Not enough yeast or too high water temperature. Possible contact of yeast with salt or insufficient room temperature.	Increase the amount of yeast and monitor the water and room temperature. Do not let the yeast come into direct contact with salt.
6	**Too much dough**	High consumption of liquid and yeast.	Reduce the amount of liquid or yeast used in the recipe.
7	**Bread loses shape during baking**	Using the wrong type of flour.	Select the flour recommended for your recipe.
		Yeast acts too quickly or the room temperature is too high.	Use yeast at room temperature and control the room temperature.
		Too much water in the dough.	Carefully adhere to the amount of water specified in the recipe; add a bit more flour.
8	**Bread is too big and has a dense structure**	Excessive use of flour and not enough water.	Adjust the proportions of flour and water.
		Too many fruits or whole grains added.	Reduce the quantity of these additions and, if necessary, increase the amount of yeast.
9	**Bread is hollow inside**	Too much water or yeast, and not enough salt.	Review the proportions of water and yeast, add more salt.
		Water was too hot.	Check and adjust the water temperature.

During normal operation, there should be no smoke or fire coming from the bread machine, nor should the bread machine make strange or excessively loud noises. In any unusual situations, damage to the bread machine, or malfunction of its components - immediately unplug the bread machine and contact the service center of your device's manufacturer. Do not leave the bread machine unattended for an extended period and do not leave it operating overnight.

ALTERNATIVE NAMES FOR CYCLES
IN DIFFERENT BREAD MACHINES

Basic: • Basic Bread • Standard • Classic Bread • Basic Mode • Basic Wheat • White	**Fruit And Nuts:** • Fruit & Nut Bread • Add-Ins • Mix-Ins • Mix Bread • Raisin Mo
Dough: • Dough • Pizza Dough • Bread Dough Preparation • Rise • Manual • Basic Dough • Quick Dou	**Whole Wheat:** • Whole Wheat • 100% Whole Wheat • Basic Wheat • Whole Grain
French Bread: • French • Artisan • French Crust • Crisp • European • Homemade	**Quick Yeast Bread:** • Quick Bread • Rapid Yeast Bread • Express Bake • Bake • Quick Bake • Quick • Rapid • Turbo

These names give a clear indication of what each mode is designed for, allowing users to easily select the right setting for their baking needs

BASIC BREAD RECIPES

BASIC WHITE BREAD

PREP TIME: 10 MINUTES
RISING TIME: 1-2 HOURS
BAKING TIME: APPROXIMATELY 1 HOUR
COMPLEXITY: BEGINNER

TOOL FUNCTION:
BREAD MAKER OPERATING SETTING:
BASIC/WHITE BREAD SETTING
BAKING TEMPERATURE: 375°F (190°C)

TOOLS NEEDED:
BREAD MAKER MEASURING
CUPS AND SPOONS

INGREDIENTS	1 POUND	1.5 POUND	2 POUND
WARM WATER	¾ cup (180 ml)	1 cup (240 ml)	1 ¼ cups (300 ml)
SUGAR	2 tbsps. (28 g)	3 tbsps. (42 g)	¼ cup (48 g)
SALT	1 ½ tsps. (9 g)	1 ½ tsps. (9 g)	1 ½ tsps. (9 g)
BREAD FLOUR	2 cups (250 g)	3 cups (375 g)	4 cups (500 g)
UNSALTED BUTTER	2 tbsps. (28 g)	2 tbsps. (28 g)	¼ cup (56 g)
ACTIVE DRY YEAST	2 tsps. (5 g)	2 tsps. (5 g)	2 tsps. (5 g)

INSTRUCTIONS

1. Load the bread maker pan with all the ingredients in the order listed, starting with combining the wet and dry components, ensuring the yeast is added last, on top of the flour.
2. Select the Basic/White Bread setting on the bread maker and choose the desired loaf size (1 pound, 1.5 pounds, or 2 pounds).
3. Start the bread maker. The process of mixing the ingredients will begin.
4. Let the dough rise in the bread maker for approximately 1 hour or until it reaches the top of the pan.
5. The bread maker will automatically start the baking cycle once the rising cycle is complete. 6. After the baking cycle, cool the bread on a wire rack after carefully removing it from the pan; then, slice it.

NUTRITION PER SERVING (1 SLICE): CALORIES 110, CARBS 20G, FAT 2G, PROTEIN 3G, FIBER 1G, SODIUM 200MG

HONEY WHITE BREAD

PREP TIME: 10 MINUTES
RISING TIME: 1-2 HOURS
BAKING TIME: APPROXIMATELY 1 HOUR
COMPLEXITY: BEGINNER

TOOL FUNCTION:
BREAD MAKER OPERATING SETTING:
BASIC/WHITE BREAD SETTING
BAKING TEMPERATURE: 375°F (190°C)

TOOLS NEEDED:
BREAD MAKER MEASURING
CUPS AND SPOONS

INGREDIENTS	1 POUND	1.5 POUND	2 POUND
WARM WATER	¾ cup (180 ml)	1 cup (240 ml)	1 ¼ cups (300 ml)
HONEY	1 tbsp. (21 g)	1.5 tbsps. (32 g)	2 tbsps. (42 g)
UNSALTED BUTTER	2 tbsps. (28 g)	2 tbsps. (28 g)	¼ cup (56 g)
SALT	1 ½ tsps. (9 g)	1 ½ tsps. (9 g)	1 ½ tsps. (9 g)
BREAD FLOUR	2 cups (250 g)	3 cups (375 g)	4 cups (500 g)
ACTIVE DRY YEAST	1 tsp. (2.5 g)	1.5 tsps. (3.75 g)	2 tsps. (5 g)

INSTRUCTIONS

1. Load the bread maker pan with all the ingredients in the order listed, starting with combining the wet and dry components, ensuring the yeast is added last, on top of the flour.
2. Select the Basic/White Bread setting on the bread maker and choose the desired loaf size (1 pound, 1.5 pounds, or 2 pounds).
3. Start the bread maker. The process of mixing the ingredients will begin.
4. Let the dough rise in the bread maker for approximately 1 hour or until it reaches the top of the pan.
5. The bread maker will automatically start the baking cycle once the rising cycle is complete.
6. After the baking cycle, cool the bread on a wire rack after carefully removing it from the pan; then, slice it.

NUTRITION PER SERVING (1 SLICE): CALORIES 110, CARBS 20G, FAT 2G, PROTEIN 3G, FIBER 1G, SODIUM 200MG

ITALIAN WHITE BREAD

PREP TIME: 10 MINUTES
RISING TIME: 1-2 HOURS
BAKING TIME: APPROXIMATELY 1 HOUR
COMPLEXITY: BEGINNER

TOOL FUNCTION:
BREAD MAKER OPERATING SETTING:
BASIC/WHITE BREAD SETTING
BAKING TEMPERATURE: 375°F (190°C)

TOOLS NEEDED:
BREAD MAKER MEASURING
CUPS AND SPOONS

INGREDIENTS	1 POUND	1.5 POUND	2 POUND
WARM WATER	¾ cup (180 ml)	1 cup (240 ml)	1 ¼ cups (300 ml)
SUGAR	1 tbsp. (14 g)	1.5 tbsps. (21 g)	2 tbsps. (28 g)
SALT	1 ½ tsps. (9 g)	1 ½ tsps. (9 g)	1 ½ tsps. (9 g)
BREAD FLOUR	2 cups (250 g)	3 cups (375 g)	4 cups (500 g)
OLIVE OIL	1 tbsp. (15 ml)	1.5 tbsps. (22.5 ml)	2 tbsps. (30 ml)
ACTIVE DRY YEAST	1 tsp. (2.5 g)	1.5 tsps. (3.75 g)	2 tsps. (5 g)

INSTRUCTIONS

1. Load the bread maker pan with all the ingredients in the order listed, starting with combining the wet and dry components, ensuring the yeast is added last, on top of the flour.
2. Select the Basic/White Bread setting on the bread maker and choose the desired loaf size (1 pound, 1.5 pounds, or 2 pounds).
3. Start the bread maker. The process of mixing the ingredients will begin.
4. Let the dough rise in the bread maker for approximately 1 hour or until it reaches the top of the pan.
5. Bread maker will automatically start the baking cycle once the rising cycle is complete.
6. After the baking cycle, cool the bread on a wire rack after carefully removing it from the pan; then, slice it.

NUTRITION PER SERVING (1 SLICE): CALORIES 120; FAT 2.5G; CARBS 20G; PROTEIN 4G; FIBER 1G; SODIUM 180MG

EGG BREAD

PREP TIME: 10 MINUTES
RISING TIME: 1-2 HOURS
BAKING TIME: APPROXIMATELY 1 HOUR
COMPLEXITY: BEGINNER

TOOL FUNCTION:
BREAD MAKER OPERATING SETTING:
BASIC/WHITE BREAD SETTING
BAKING TEMPERATURE: 375°F (190°C)

TOOLS NEEDED:
BREAD MAKER
MEASURING CUPS AND
SPOON

INGREDIENTS	1 POUND	1.5 POUND	2 POUND
WARM WATER	½ cup (120 ml)	¾ cup (180 ml)	1 cup (240 ml)
LARGE EGG	1	1	2
UNSALTED BUTTER	2 tbsps. (28 g)	3 tbsps. (42 g)	4 tbsps. (56 g)
SUGAR	1 tbsp. (12 g)	1.5 tbsps. (18 g)	2 tbsps. (24 g)
SALT	1 tsp. (3 g)	1.5 tsps. (4 g)	2 tsps. (5 g)
BREAD FLOUR	1 ½ cups (188 g)	2 ¼ cups (281 g)	3 cups (375 g)
ACTIVE DRY YEAST	1 tsp. (2.5 g)	1.5 tsps. (3.75 g)	2 tsps. (5 g)

INSTRUCTIONS

1. Load the bread maker pan with all the ingredients in the order listed, starting with combining the wet and dry components, ensuring the yeast is added last, on top of the flour.
2. Select the Basic/White Bread setting on the bread maker and choose the desired loaf size (1 pound, 1.5 pounds, or 2 pounds).
3. Start the bread maker. The process of mixing the ingredients will begin.
4. Let the dough rise in the bread maker for approximately 1 hour, or until it reaches the top of the pan.
5. The bread maker will automatically start the baking cycle once the rising cycle is complete.
6. After the baking cycle, cool the bread on a wire rack after carefully removing it from the pan; then, slice it.

NUTRITION PER SERVING (1 SLICE): CALORIES 130, FAT 5G, CARBS 17G, PROTEIN 4G, FIBER 1G, SODIUM 200MG

LIGHT RYE BREAD

PREP TIME: 10 MINUTES
RISING TIME: 1-2 HOURS
BAKING TIME: APPROXIMATELY 1 HOUR
COMPLEXITY: BEGINNER

TOOL FUNCTION:
BREAD MAKER OPERATING SETTING:
BASIC/WHITE BREAD SETTING
BAKING TEMPERATURE: 375°F (190°C)

TOOLS NEEDED:
BREAD MAKER
MEASURING CUPS AND
SPOONS

INGREDIENTS	1 POUND	1.5 POUND	2 POUND
WARM WATER	¾ cup (180 ml)	1 cup (240 ml)	1 ¼ cups (300 ml)
HONEY	1 tbsp. (21 g)	1.5 tbsps. (32 g)	2 tbsps. (42 g)
UNSALTED BUTTER	1 tbsp. (14 g)	1.5 tbsps. (21 g)	2 tbsps. (28 g)
SALT	1 tsp. (5 g)	1.5 tsps. (7.5 g)	2 tsps. (10 g)
BREAD FLOUR	1 cup (125 g)	1 ½ cups (188 g)	2 cups (250 g)
RYE FLOUR	1 cup (125 g)	1 ½ cups (188 g)	2 cups (250 g)
CARAWAY SEEDS	1 tsp. (2.5 g)	1 ½ tsps. (3.75 g)	2 tsps. (5 g)
ACTIVE DRY YEAST	1 tsp. (2.5 g)	1 ½ tsps. (3.75 g)	2 tsps. (5 g)

INSTRUCTIONS

1. Put everything in the bread maker pan in the order listed, starting with liquids before adding dry ingredients, ensuring the yeast is added last, on top of the flour.
2. Select the Basic/White Bread setting on the bread maker and choose the desired loaf size (1 pound, 1.5 pounds, or 2 pounds).
3. Start the bread maker. The process of mixing the ingredients will begin.
4. Let the dough rise in the bread maker for approximately 1 hour or until it reaches the top of the pan.
5. The bread maker will automatically start the baking cycle once the rising cycle is complete.
6. After the baking cycle, carefully slice the bread after cooling on a wire rack.

NUTRITION PER SERVING (1 SLICE): CALORIES 110; FAT 1.5G; CARBS 20G; PROTEIN 3G; FIBER 2G; SODIUM 180MG

SOUR CREAM CORNMEAL BREAD

PREP TIME: 10 MINUTES
RISING TIME: 1-2 HOURS
BAKING TIME: APPROXIMATELY 1 HOUR
COMPLEXITY: BEGINNER

TOOL FUNCTION:
BREAD MAKER OPERATING SETTING:
BASIC/WHITE BREAD SETTING
BAKING TEMPERATURE: 375°F (190°C)

TOOLS NEEDED:
BREAD MAKER
MEASURING CUPS AND
SPOON

INGREDIENTS	1 POUND	1.5 POUND	2 POUND
WARM WATER	¾ cup (180 ml)	1 cup (240 ml)	1 ¼ cups (300 ml)
SOUR CREAM	¼ cup (60 g)	⅓ cup (80 g)	½ cup (120 g)
UNSALTED BUTTER	2 tbsps. (28 g)	3 tbsps. (42 g)	¼ cup (56 g)
HONEY	2 tbsps. (30 g)	3 tbsps. (45 g)	¼ cup (60 g)
SALT	1 tsp. (5 g)	1 ½ tsps. (7.5 g)	2 tsps. (10 g)
BREAD FLOUR	1 ½ cups (188 g)	2 ¼ cups (281 g)	3 cups (375 g)
CORNMEAL	½ cups (60 g)	¾ cups (90 g)	1 cups (120 g)
ACTIVE DRY YEAST	1 tsp. (2.5 g)	1 ½ tsps. (3.75 g)	2 tsps. (5 g)

INSTRUCTIONS

1. Put everything in the bread maker pan in the order listed, starting with liquids before adding dry ingredients, ensuring the yeast is added last, on top of the flour.
2. Select the Basic/White Bread setting on the bread maker and choose the desired loaf size (1 pound, 1.5 pounds, or 2 pounds).
3. Start the bread maker. The process of mixing the ingredients will begin.
4. Let the dough rise in the bread maker for approximately 1 hour or until it reaches the top of the pan.
5. The bread maker will automatically start the baking cycle once the rising cycle is complete.
6. After the baking cycle, carefully slice the bread after cooling on a wire rack.

NUTRITION PER SERVING (1 SLICE): CALORIES 120, FAT 4G, CARBS 18G, PROTEIN 3G, FIBER 1G, SODIUM 180MG

CLASSIC BLACK BREAD

PREP TIME: 10 MINUTES
RISING TIME: 1-2 HOURS
BAKING TIME: APPROXIMATELY 1 HOUR
COMPLEXITY: BEGINNER

TOOL FUNCTION:
BREAD MAKER OPERATING SETTING:
BASIC/WHITE BREAD SETTING
BAKING TEMPERATURE: 375°F (190°C)

TOOLS NEEDED:
BREAD MAKER
MEASURING CUPS AND
SPOON

INGREDIENTS	1 POUND	1.5 POUND	2 POUND
WARM WATER	¾ cup (180 ml)	1 cup (240 ml)	1 ¼ cups (300 ml)
MOLASSES	2 tbsps. (28 g)	3 tbsps. (42 g)	4 tbsps. (56 g)
VEGETABLE OIL	1 tbsp. (15 ml)	1.5 tbsps. (22.5 ml)	2 tbsps. (30 ml)
SALT	1 tsp. (5 g)	1.5 tsps. (7.5 g)	2 tsps. (10 g)
BREAD FLOUR	1 cup (125 g)	1 ½ cups (188 g)	2 cups (250 g)
RYE FLOUR	1 cup (125 g)	1 ½ cups (188 g)	2 cups (250 g)
COCOA POWDER	1 tbsp. (10 g)	1 ½ tbsps. (15 g)	2 tbsps. (20 g)
CARAWAY SEEDS	1 tsp. (2.5 g)	1 ½ tsps. (3.75 g)	2 tsps. (5 g)
ACTIVE DRY YEAST	1 tsp. (2.5 g)	1 ½ tsps. (3.75 g)	2 tsps. (5 g)

INSTRUCTIONS

1. Fill the bread machine pan with all the ingredients in the order listed, starting with combining the liquids, followed by the dry ingredients, ensuring the yeast is added last, on top of the flour.
2. Select the Basic/White Bread setting on the bread maker and choose the desired loaf size (1 pound, 1.5 pounds, or 2 pounds).
3. Start the bread maker. The process of mixing the ingredients will begin.
4. Let the dough rise in the bread maker for approximately 1 hour or until it reaches the top of the pan.
5. The bread maker will automatically start the baking cycle once the rising cycle is complete.
6. After the baking cycle, before slicing, cool on a wire rack when it has been removed from the pan.

NUTRITION PER SERVING (1 SLICE): CALORIES 110; 2G FAT; 20G CARBOHYDRATES; 3G PROTEIN; 2G FIBER; SODIUM 180MG

IRISH SODA BREAD

PREP TIME: 10 MINUTES
RISING TIME: 1-2 HOURS
BAKING TIME: APPROXIMATELY 1 HOUR
COMPLEXITY: BEGINNER

TOOL FUNCTION:
BREAD MAKER OPERATING SETTING:
QUICK BREAD SETTING
BAKING TEMPERATURE: 375°F (190°C)

TOOLS NEEDED:
BREAD MAKER
MEASURING CUPS AND
SPOONS

INGREDIENTS	1 POUND	1.5 POUND	2 POUND
BUTTERMILK	1 cup (240 ml)	1 ½ cups (360 ml)	2 cups (480 ml)
UNSALTED BUTTER	2 tbsps. (28 g)	3 tbsps. (42 g)	¼ cup (56 g)
ALL-PURPOSE FLOUR	2 cups (250 g)	3 cups (375 g)	4 cups (500 g)
GRANULATED SUGAR	1 tbsp. (12 g)	1 ½ tbsps. (18 g)	2 tbsps. (24 g)
BAKING SODA	½ tsp. (3 g)	¾ tsp. (4.5 g)	1 tsp. (6 g)
SALT	½ tsp. (3 g)	¾ tsp. (4.5 g)	1 tsp. (6 g)

INSTRUCTIONS

1. Fill the bread machine pan with all the ingredients in the order listed, starting with combining the liquids, followed by the dry ingredients, ensuring the yeast is added last, on top of the flour.
2. Select the Quick Bread setting on the bread maker and choose the desired loaf size (1 pound, 1.5 pounds, or 2 pounds).
3. Start the bread maker. The process of mixing the ingredients will begin.
4. Let the dough rise in the bread maker for approximately 1 hour or until it reaches the top of the pan.
5. The bread maker will automatically start the baking cycle once the rising cycle is complete.
6. After the baking cycle, before slicing, cool on a wire rack when it has been removed from the pan.

NUTRITION PER SERVING (1 SLICE): CALORIES 150; FAT 3G; CARBS 28G; PROTEIN 4G; FIBER 2G; SODIUM 300MG

ANADAMA BREAD

PREP TIME: 10 MINUTES
RISING TIME: 1-2 HOURS
BAKING TIME: APPROXIMATELY 1 HOUR
COMPLEXITY: BEGINNER

TOOL FUNCTION:
BREAD MAKER OPERATING SETTING:
BASIC/WHITE BREAD SETTING
BAKING TEMPERATURE: 375°F (190°C)

TOOLS NEEDED:
BREAD MAKER
MEASURING CUPS AND
SPOONS

INGREDIENTS	1 POUND	1.5 POUND	2 POUND
WARM WATER	¾ cup (180 ml)	1 cup (240 ml)	1 ¼ cups (300 ml)
MOLASSES	2 tbsps. (28 g)	3 tbsps. (42 g)	4 tbsps. (56 g)
VEGETABLE OIL	1 tbsp. (15 ml)	1.5 tbsps. (22.5 ml)	2 tbsps. (30 ml)
SALT	1 tsp. (5 g)	1.5 tsps. (7.5 g)	2 tsps. (10 g)
BREAD FLOUR	1 cup (125 g)	1 ½ cups (188 g)	2 cups (250 g)
RYE FLOUR	1 cup (125 g)	1 ½ cups (188 g)	2 cups (250 g)
COCOA POWDER	¼ cup (30 g)	⅓ cup (40 g)	½ cup (60 g)
CARAWAY SEEDS	1 tbsp. (15 g)	1 ½ tbsps. (22.5 g)	2 tbsps. (30 g)
INSTANT COFFEE GRANULES	1 tsp. (2.5 g)	1 ½ tsps. (3.75 g)	2 tsps. (5 g)
ACTIVE DRY YEAST	1 tsp. (2.5 g)	1 ½ tsps. (3.75 g)	2 tsps. (5 g)

INSTRUCTIONS

1. Fill the bread machine pan with all the ingredients in the order listed, starting with combining the liquids, followed by the dry ingredients, ensuring the yeast is added last, on top of the flour.
2. Select the Basic/White Bread setting on the bread maker and choose the desired loaf size (1 pound, 1.5 pounds, or 2 pounds).
3. Start the bread maker. The process of mixing the ingredients will begin.
4. Let the dough rise in the bread maker for approximately 1 hour or until it reaches the top of the pan.
5. The bread maker will automatically start the baking cycle once the rising cycle is complete.
6. After the baking cycle, before slicing, cool on a wire rack when it has been removed from the pan.

- -

NUTRITION PER SERVING (1 SLICE): CALORIES 130; FAT 2G; CARBS 25G; PROTEIN 4G; FIBER 2G; SODIUM 200MG

SALLY LUNN BREAD

PREP TIME: 10 MINUTES
RISING TIME: 1-2 HOURS
BAKING TIME: APPROXIMATELY 1 HOUR
COMPLEXITY: BEGINNER

TOOL FUNCTION:
BREAD MAKER OPERATING SETTING:
BASIC/WHITE BREAD SETTING
BAKING TEMPERATURE: 375°F (190°C)

TOOLS NEEDED:
BREAD MAKER
MEASURING CUPS AND
SPOONS

INGREDIENTS	1 POUND	1.5 POUND	2 POUND
WARM MILK	¾ cup (180 ml)	1 cup (240 ml)	1 ¼ cups (300 ml)
WARM WATER	¼ cup (60 ml)	⅓ cup (80 ml)	½ cup (120 ml)
LARGE EGGS	2	3	4
UNSALTED BUTTER	¼ cup (56 g)	⅓ cup (75 g)	½ cup (113 g)
GRANULATED SUGAR	2 tbsps. (25 g)	3 tbsps. (37.5 g)	½ cup (100 g)
BREAD FLOUR	3 cups (375 g)	4 ½ cups (563 g)	6 cups (750 g)
SALT	1 tsp. (5 g)	1 ½ tsps. (7.5 g)	2 tsps. (10 g)
ACTIVE DRY YEAST	2 tsps. (6 g)	3 tsps. (9 g)	4 tsps. (12 g)

INSTRUCTIONS

1. Fill the bread maker pan with all the ingredients in the order listed, starting with combining the liquids, followed by the dry ingredients, ensuring the yeast is added last, on top of the flour.
2. Select the Basic/White Bread setting on the bread maker and choose the desired loaf size (1 pound, 1.5 pounds, or 2 pounds).
3. Start the bread maker. The process of mixing the ingredients will begin.
4. Let the dough rise in the bread maker for approximately 1 hour or until it reaches the top of the pan.
5. The bread maker will automatically start the baking cycle once the rising cycle is complete.
6. After the baking cycle, before slicing, cool on a wire rack when it has been removed from the pan.

- -

NUTRITION PER SERVING (1 SLICE): CALORIES 150; PROTEIN 4G; FAT 5G; CARBS 22G; FIBER 1G; SODIUM 200MG

BEER MUSTARD BREAD

PREP TIME: 10 MINUTES
RISING TIME: 1-2 HOURS
BAKING TIME: APPROXIMATELY 1 HOUR
COMPLEXITY: BEGINNER

TOOL FUNCTION:
BREAD MAKER OPERATING SETTING:
BASIC/WHITE BREAD SETTING
BAKING TEMPERATURE: 375°F (190°C)

TOOLS NEEDED:
BREAD MAKER
MEASURING CUPS AND
SPOONS

INGREDIENTS	1 POUND	1.5 POUND	2 POUND
WARM BEER	½ cup (120 ml)	¾ cup (180 ml)	1 cup (240 ml)
OLIVE OIL	2 tbsps. (30 ml)	3 tbsps. (45 ml)	¼ cup (60 ml)
WHOLE-GRAIN MUSTARD	2 tbsps. (30 g)	3 tbsps. (45 g)	¼ cup (60 g)
HONEY	1 tbsp. (15 g)	1 ½ tbsps. (22.5 g)	2 tbsps. (30 g)
SALT	1 tsp. (5 g)	1 ½ tsps. (9 g)	2 tsps. (12 g)
BREAD FLOUR	2 ¼ cups (282 g)	3 ½ cups (438 g)	4 cups (500 g)
ACTIVE DRY YEAST	1 tsp. (3 g)	1 ½ tsps. (4.5 g)	2 tsps. (6 g)

INSTRUCTIONS

1. Fill the bread maker pan with all the ingredients in the order listed, starting with combining the liquids, followed by the dry ingredients, ensuring the yeast is added last, on top of the flour.
2. Select the Basic/White Bread setting on the bread maker and choose the desired loaf size (1 pound, 1.5 pounds, or 2 pounds).
3. Start the bread maker. The process of mixing the ingredients will begin.
4. Let the dough rise in the bread maker for approximately 1 hour or until it reaches the top of the pan.
5. The bread maker will automatically start the baking cycle once the rising cycle is complete.
6. After the baking cycle, before slicing, cool on a wire rack when it has been removed from the pan.

NUTRITION PER SERVING (1 SLICE): CALORIES 140; PROTEIN 4G; FAT 2.5G; CARBS 25G; FIBER 1G; SODIUM 220MG

WHOLE MILK WHITE BREAD

PREP TIME: 10 MINUTES
RISING TIME: 1-2 HOURS
BAKING TIME: APPROXIMATELY 1 HOUR
COMPLEXITY: BEGINNER

TOOL FUNCTION:
BREAD MAKER OPERATING SETTING:
FRENCH
BREAD SETTING OR BASIC/WHITE
BREAD SETTINGN
BAKING TEMPERATURE: 375°F (190°C)

TOOLS NEEDED:
BREAD MAKER
MEASURING CUPS AND
SPOONS

INGREDIENTS	1 POUND	1.5 POUND	2 POUND
WHOLE MILK	¾ cup (180 ml)	1 ⅛ cup (270 ml)	1 ½ cups (360 ml)
GRANULATED SUGAR	1.5 tbsps. (19 g)	3 tbsps. (38 g)	4 tbsps. (50 g)
SALT	½ tsp. (3 g)	¾ tsp. (4.5 g)	1 tsp. (6 g)
UNSALTED BUTTER	1.5 tbsps. (21 g)	3 tbsps. (42 g)	4 tbsps. (56 g)
BREAD FLOUR	2.25 cups (270 g)	3.2 cups (405 g)	4.5 cups (540 g)
ACTIVE DRY YEAST	1.5 tsps. (5 g)	2.25 tsps. (7.5 g)	3 tsps. (10.5 g)

INSTRUCTIONS

1. Fill the bread machine pan with all the ingredients in the order listed, starting with combining the liquids, followed by the dry ingredients, ensuring the yeast is added last, on top of the flour.
2. Select the Basic/White Bread setting on the bread maker and choose the desired loaf size (1 pound, 1.5 pounds, or 2 pounds).
3. Start the bread maker. The process of mixing the ingredients will begin.
4. Let the dough rise in the bread maker for approximately 1 hour or until it reaches the top of the pan.
5. The bread maker will automatically start the baking cycle once the rising cycle is complete.
6. After the baking cycle, before slicing, cool on a wire rack when it has been removed from the pan.

NUTRITION PER SERVING (1 SLICE): CALORIES 110; PROTEIN 3G; FAT 1G; CARBS 22G; FIBER 1G; SODIUM 180MG

SWEDISH LIMPA BREAD

PREP TIME: 10 MINUTES
RISING TIME: 1-2 HOURS
BAKING TIME: APPROXIMATELY 1 HOUR
COMPLEXITY: BEGINNER

TOOL FUNCTION:
BREAD MAKER OPERATING SETTING:
BASIC/WHITE BREAD SETTING
BAKING TEMPERATURE: 375°F (190°C)

TOOLS NEEDED:
BREAD MAKER
MEASURING CUPS AND
SPOONS

INGREDIENTS	1 POUND	1.5 POUND	2 POUND
WARM WATER	¾ cup (180 ml)	1 cup (240 ml)	1 ¼ cups (300 ml)
MOLASSES	2 tbsps. (28 g)	3 tbsps. (42 g)	4 tbsps. (56 g)
VEGETABLE OIL	1 tbsp. (15 ml)	1.5 tbsps. (22.5 ml)	2 tbsps. (30 ml)
SALT	1 tsp. (5 g)	1.5 tsps. (7.5 g)	2 tsps. (10 g)
BREAD FLOUR	1 cup (125 g)	1 ½ cups (188 g)	2 cups (250 g)
RYE FLOUR	1 cup (125 g)	1 ½ cups (188 g)	2 cups (250 g)
ORANGE ZEST	1 tbsp. (15 g)	1 ½ tbsps. (22.5 g)	2 tbsps. (30 g)
CARAWAY SEEDS	1 tbsp. (15 g)	1 ½ tbsps. (22.5 g)	2 tbsps. (30 g)
ACTIVE DRY YEAST	1 tsp. (2.5 g)	1 ½ tsps. (3.75 g)	2 tsps. (5 g)

INSTRUCTIONS

1. Fill the bread maker pan with all the ingredients in the order listed, starting with combining the liquids, followed by the dry ingredients, ensuring the yeast is added last, on top of the flour.
2. Select the Basic/White Bread setting on the bread maker and choose the desired loaf size (1 pound, 1.5 pounds, or 2 pounds).
3. Start the bread maker. The process of mixing the ingredients will begin.
4. Let the dough rise in the bread maker for approximately 1 hour or until it reaches the top of the pan.
5. The bread maker will automatically start the baking cycle once the rising cycle is complete.
6. After the baking cycle, before slicing, cool on a wire rack when it has been removed from the pan.

NUTRITION PER SERVING (1 SLICE): CALORIES 110; FAT 1.5G; CARBS 22G; PROTEIN 3G; FIBER 2G; SODIUM 180MG

WHOLE GRAIN WHITE BREAD

WHOLE GRAIN WHITE BREAD

PREP TIME: 10 MINUTES
RISING TIME: 1-2 HOURS
BAKING TIME: APPROXIMATELY 1 HOUR
COMPLEXITY: BEGINNER

TOOL FUNCTION:
BREAD MAKER OPERATING SETTING:
BASIC/WHITE BREAD SETTING
BAKING TEMPERATURE: 375°F (190°C)

TOOLS NEEDED:
BREAD MAKER
MEASURING CUPS AND SPOONS

INGREDIENTS	1 POUND	1.5 POUND	2 POUND
WARM WATER	¾ cup (180 ml)	1 cup (240 ml)	1 ¼ cups (300 ml)
OLIVE OIL	2 tbsp. (30 ml)	3 tbsp. (45 ml)	4 tbsp. (60 ml)
HONEY	2 tbsp. (30 ml)	3 tbsp. (45 ml)	4 tbsp. (60 ml)
SALT	1 tsp. (5 g)	1 ½ tsp. (7.5 g)	2 tsp. (10 g)
WHOLE WHEAT FLOUR	1 ½ cups (180 g)	2 ¼ cups (270 g)	3 cups (360 g)
BREAD FLOUR	½ cup (60 g)	¾ cup (90 g)	1 cup (120 g)
ACTIVE DRY YEAST	1 ½ tsp. (4.5 g)	2 tsp. (6 g)	2 ½ tsp. (7.5 g)

INSTRUCTIONS

1. Fill the bread machine pan with all the ingredients in the order listed, starting with combining the liquids, followed by the dry ingredients, ensuring the yeast is added last, on top of the flour.
2. Select the Basic/White Bread setting on the bread maker and choose the desired loaf size (1 pound, 1.5 pounds, or 2 pounds).
3. Start the bread maker. The process of mixing the ingredients will begin.
4. Let the dough rise in the bread maker for approximately 1 hour or until it reaches the top of the pan.
5. The bread maker will automatically start the baking cycle once the rising cycle is complete.
6. After the baking cycle, before slicing, cool on a wire rack when it has been removed from the pan.

NUTRITION PER SERVING (1 SLICE): CALORIES 120; PROTEIN 4G; FAT 2G; CARBS 23G; FIBER 3G; SODIUM 180MG

WHOLE GRAIN WHITE BREAD WITH OATS

PREP TIME: 10 MINUTES
RISING TIME: 1-2 HOURS
BAKING TIME: APPROXIMATELY 1 HOUR
COMPLEXITY: BEGINNER

TOOL FUNCTION:
BREAD MAKER OPERATING SETTING:
BASIC/ WHITE BREAD SETTING
BAKING TEMPERATURE: 375°F (190°C)

TOOLS NEEDED:
BREAD MAKER
MEASURING CUPS AND
SPOONS

INGREDIENTS	1 POUND	1.5 POUND	2 POUND
WARM WATER	¾ cup (180 ml)	1 cup (240 ml)	1 ¼ cups (300 ml)
OLIVE OIL	2 tbsp. (30 ml)	3 tbsp. (45 ml)	4 tbsp. (60 ml)
HONEY	2 tbsp. (30 ml)	3 tbsp. (45 ml)	4 tbsp. (60 ml)
SALT	1 tsp. (5 g)	1 ½ tsp. (7.5 g)	2 tsp. (10 g)
WHOLE WHEAT FLOUR	1 cup (120 g)	1 ½ cups (180 g)	2 cups (240 g)
BREAD FLOUR	½ cup (60 g)	¾ cup (90 g)	1 cup (120 g)
ROLLED OATS	¼ cup (30 g)	⅓ cup (40 g)	½ cup (60 g)
ACTIVE DRY YEAST	1 ½ tsp. (4.5 g)	2 tsp. (6 g)	2 ½ tsp. (7.5 g)

INSTRUCTIONS

1. Fill the bread maker pan with all the ingredients in the order listed, starting with combining the liquids, followed by the dry ingredients, ensuring the yeast is added last, on top of the flour.
2. Select the Basic/White Bread setting on the bread maker and choose the desired loaf size (1 pound, 1.5 pounds, or 2 pounds).
3. Start the bread maker. The process of mixing the ingredients will begin.
4. Allow the dough to rise in the bread maker for approximately 1 hour or until it reaches the top of the pan.
5. The bread maker will automatically start the baking cycle once the rising cycle is complete.
6. After the baking cycle, before slicing, cool on a wire rack when it has been removed from the pan.

NUTRITION PER SERVING (1 SLICE): CALORIES 140; PROTEIN 4G; FAT 3G; CARBS 25G; FIBER 4G; SODIUM 190MG

WHOLE GRAIN WHITE BREAD WITH FLAXSEEDS

PREP TIME: 10 MINUTES
RISING TIME: 1-2 HOURS
BAKING TIME: APPROXIMATELY 1 HOUR
COMPLEXITY: BEGINNER

TOOL FUNCTION:
BREAD MAKER OPERATING SETTING:
BASIC/WHITE BREAD SETTING
BAKING TEMPERATURE: 375°F (190°C)

TOOLS NEEDED:
BREAD MAKER
MEASURING CUPS AND
SPOONS

INGREDIENTS	1 POUND	1.5 POUND	2 POUND
WARM WATER	¾ cup (180 ml)	1 cup (240 ml)	1 ¼ cups (300 ml)
OLIVE OIL	2 tbsp. (30 ml)	3 tbsp. (45 ml)	4 tbsp. (60 ml)
HONEY	2 tbsp. (30 ml)	3 tbsp. (45 ml)	4 tbsp. (60 ml)
SALT	1 tsp. (5 g)	1 ½ tsp. (7.5 g)	2 tsp. (10 g)
WHOLE WHEAT FLOUR	1 cup (120 g)	1 ½ cups (180 g)	2 cups (240 g)
BREAD FLOUR	½ cup (60 g)	¾ cup (90 g)	1 cup (120 g)
GROUND FLAX SEEDS	¼ cup (30 g)	⅓ cup (40 g)	½ cup (60 g)
ACTIVE DRY YEAST	1 ½ tsp. (4.5 g)	2 tsp. (6 g)	2 ½ tsp. (7.5 g)

INSTRUCTIONS

1. Fill the bread machine pan with all the ingredients in the order listed, starting with combining the liquids, followed by the dry ingredients, ensuring the yeast is added last, on top of the flour.
2. Select the Basic/White Bread setting on the bread maker and choose the desired loaf size (1 pound, 1.5 pounds, or 2 pounds).
3. Start the bread maker. The process of mixing the ingredients will begin.
4. Allow the dough to rise in the bread maker for approximately 1 hour or until it reaches the top of the pan.
5. The bread maker will automatically start the baking cycle once the rising cycle is complete.
6. After the baking cycle, before slicing, cool on a wire rack when it has been removed from the pan.

NUTRITION PER SERVING (1 SLICE): CALORIES 130; PROTEIN 4G; FAT 3G; CARBS 24G; FIBER 4G; SODIUM 190MG

MULTI-GRAIN WHITE BREAD

PREP TIME: 10 MINUTES
RISING TIME: 1-2 HOURS
BAKING TIME: APPROXIMATELY 1 HOUR
COMPLEXITY: BEGINNER

TOOL FUNCTION:
BREAD MAKER OPERATING SETTING:
BASIC/ WHITE BREAD SETTING
BAKING TEMPERATURE: 375°F (190°C)

TOOLS NEEDED:
BREAD MAKER
MEASURING CUPS AND
SPOONS

INGREDIENTS	1 POUND	1.5 POUND	2 POUND
WARM WATER	¾ cup (180 ml)	1 cup (240 ml)	1 ¼ cups (300 ml)
OLIVE OIL	2 tbsp. (30 ml)	3 tbsp. (45 ml)	4 tbsp. (60 ml)
HONEY	2 tbsp. (30 ml)	3 tbsp. (45 ml)	4 tbsp. (60 ml)
SALT	1 tsp. (5 g)	1 ½ tsp. (7.5 g)	2 tsp. (10 g)
WHOLE WHEAT FLOUR	1 cup (120 g)	1 ½ cups (180 g)	2 cups (240 g)
BREAD FLOUR	½ cup (60 g)	¾ cup (90 g)	1 cup (120 g)
ROLLED OATS	¼ cup (30 g)	⅓ cup (40 g)	½ cup (60 g)
CORNMEAL	¼ cup (30 g)	⅓ cup (40 g)	½ cup (60 g)
FLAXSEEDS	2 tbsp. (20 g)	3 tbsp. (30 g)	¼ cup (40 g)
ACTIVE DRY YEAST	1 ½ tsp. (4.5 g)	2 tsp. (6 g)	2 ½ tsp. (7.5 g)

INSTRUCTIONS

1. Fill the bread maker pan with all the ingredients in the order listed, starting with combining the liquids, followed by the dry ingredients, ensuring the yeast is added last, on top of the flour.
2. Select the Basic/White Bread setting on the bread maker and choose the desired loaf size (1 pound, 1.5 pounds, or 2 pounds).
3. Start the bread maker. The process of mixing the ingredients will begin.
4. Allow the dough to rise in the bread maker for approximately 1 hour or until it reaches the top of the pan.
5. The bread maker will automatically start the baking cycle once the rising cycle is complete.
6. After the baking cycle, before slicing, cool on a wire rack when it has been removed from the pan.

NUTRITION PER SERVING (1 SLICE): CALORIES 140; PROTEIN 5G; FAT 3G; CARBS 25G; FIBER 4G; SODIUM 190MG

WHOLE GRAIN WHITE BREAD WITH SUNFLOWER SEEDS

PREP TIME: 10 MINUTES
RISING TIME: 1-2 HOURS
BAKING TIME: APPROXIMATELY 1 HOUR
COMPLEXITY: BEGINNER

TOOL FUNCTION:
BREAD MAKER OPERATING SETTING:
BASIC/WHITE BREAD SETTING
BAKING TEMPERATURE: 375°F (190°C)

TOOLS NEEDED:
BREAD MAKER
MEASURING CUPS AND
SPOONS

INGREDIENTS	1 POUND	1.5 POUND	2 POUND
WARM WATER	¾ cup (180 ml)	1 cup (240 ml)	1 ¼ cups (300 ml)
OLIVE OIL	2 tbsp. (30 ml)	3 tbsp. (45 ml)	4 tbsp. (60 ml)
HONEY	2 tbsp. (30 ml)	3 tbsp. (45 ml)	4 tbsp. (60 ml)
SALT	1 tsp. (5 g)	1 ½ tsp. (7.5 g)	2 tsp. (10 g)
WHOLE WHEAT FLOUR	1 cup (120 g)	1 ½ cups (180 g)	2 cups (240 g)
BREAD FLOUR	½ cup (60 g)	¾ cup (90 g)	1 cup (120 g)
SUNFLOWER SEEDS	¼ cup (30 g)	⅓ cup (40 g)	½ cup (60 g)
ACTIVE DRY YEAST	1 ½ tsp. (4.5 g)	2 tsp. (6 g)	2 ½ tsp. (7.5 g)

INSTRUCTIONS

1. Fill the bread maker pan with all the ingredients in the order listed, starting with combining the liquids, followed by the dry ingredients, ensuring the yeast is added last, on top of the flour.
2. Select the Basic/White Bread setting on the bread maker and choose the desired loaf size (1 pound, 1.5 pounds, or 2 pounds).
3. Start the bread maker. The process of mixing the ingredients will begin.
4. Allow the dough to rise in the bread maker for approximately 1 hour or until it reaches the top of the pan.
5. The bread maker will automatically start the baking cycle once the rising cycle is complete.
6. After the baking cycle, bread should be carefully taken out of the pan and allowed to cool on a wire rack before being sliced.

NUTRITION PER SERVING (1 SLICE): CALORIES 140; PROTEIN 5G; FAT 4G; CARBS 23G; FIBER 4G; SODIUM 180MG

WHOLE GRAIN WHITE BREAD WITH CHIA SEEDS

PREP TIME: 10 MINUTES
RISING TIME: 1-2 HOURS
BAKING TIME: APPROXIMATELY 1 HOUR
COMPLEXITY: BEGINNER

TOOL FUNCTION:
BREAD MAKER OPERATING SETTING:
BASIC/ WHITE BREAD SETTING
BAKING TEMPERATURE: 375°F (190°C)

TOOLS NEEDED:
BREAD MAKER
MEASURING CUPS AND
SPOONS

INGREDIENTS	1 POUND	1.5 POUND	2 POUND
WARM WATER	¾ cup (180 ml)	1 cup (240 ml)	1 ¼ cups (300 ml)
OLIVE OIL	2 tbsp. (30 ml)	3 tbsp. (45 ml)	4 tbsp. (60 ml)
HONEY	2 tbsp. (30 ml)	3 tbsp. (45 ml)	4 tbsp. (60 ml)
SALT	1 tsp. (5 g)	1 ½ tsp. (7.5 g)	2 tsp. (10 g)
WHOLE WHEAT FLOUR	1 cup (120 g)	1 ½ cups (180 g)	2 cups (240 g)
BREAD FLOUR	½ cup (60 g)	¾ cup (90 g)	1 cup (120 g)
CHIA SEEDS	2 tbsp. (30 g)	3 tbsp. (45 g)	¼ cup (60 g)
ACTIVE DRY YEAST	1 ½ tsp. (4.5 g)	2 tsp. (6 g)	2 ½ tsp. (7.5 g)

INSTRUCTIONS

1. Fill the bread machine pan with all the ingredients in the order listed, starting with combining the liquids, followed by the dry ingredients, ensuring the yeast is added last, on top of the flour.
2. Select the Basic/White Bread setting on the bread maker and choose the desired loaf size (1 pound, 1.5 pounds, or 2 pounds).
3. Start the bread maker. The process of mixing the ingredients will begin.
4. Allow the dough to rise in the bread maker for approximately 1 hour or until it reaches the top of the pan.
5. The bread maker will automatically start the baking cycle once the rising cycle is complete.
6. After the baking cycle, before slicing, cool on a wire rack when it has been removed from the pan.

NUTRITION PER SERVING (1 SLICE): CALORIES 140; PROTEIN 5G; FAT 4G; CARBS 23G; FIBER 5G; SODIUM 180MG

WHOLE GRAIN WHITE BREAD WITH WHEAT GERM

PREP TIME: 10 MINUTES
RISING TIME: 1-2 HOURS
BAKING TIME: APPROXIMATELY 1 HOUR
COMPLEXITY: BEGINNER

TOOL FUNCTION:
BREAD MAKER OPERATING SETTING:
BASIC/ WHITE BREAD SETTING
BAKING TEMPERATURE: 375°F (190°C)

TOOLS NEEDED:
BREAD MAKER
MEASURING CUPS AND
SPOONS

INGREDIENTS	1 POUND	1.5 POUND	2 POUND
WARM WATER	¾ cup (180 ml)	1 cup (240 ml)	1 ¼ cups (300 ml)
OLIVE OIL	2 tbsp. (30 ml)	3 tbsp. (45 ml)	4 tbsp. (60 ml)
HONEY	2 tbsp. (30 ml)	3 tbsp. (45 ml)	4 tbsp. (60 ml)
SALT	1 tsp. (5 g)	1 ½ tsp. (7.5 g)	2 tsp. (10 g)
WHOLE WHEAT FLOUR	1 cup (120 g)	1 ½ cups (180 g)	2 cups (240 g)
BREAD FLOUR	½ cup (60 g)	¾ cup (90 g)	1 cup (120 g)
WHEAT GERM	¼ cup (30 g)	⅓ cup (40 g)	½ cup (60 g)
ACTIVE DRY YEAST	1 ½ tsp. (4.5 g)	2 tsp. (6 g)	2 ½ tsp. (7.5 g)

INSTRUCTIONS

1. Fill the bread maker pan with all the ingredients in the order listed, starting with combining the liquids, followed by the dry ingredients, ensuring the yeast is added last, on top of the flour.
2. Select the Basic/White Bread setting on the bread maker and choose the desired loaf size (1 pound, 1.5 pounds, or 2 pounds).
3. Start the bread maker. The process of mixing the ingredients will begin.
4. Allow the dough to rise in the bread maker for approximately 1 hour or until it reaches the top of the pan.
5. The bread maker will automatically start the baking cycle once the rising cycle is complete.
6. After the baking cycle, before slicing, cool on a wire rack when it has been removed from the pan.

NUTRITION PER SERVING (1 SLICE): CALORIES 140; PROTEIN 5G; FAT 3G; CARBS 24G; FIBER 4G; SODIUM 180MG

ALMOND WHOLE GRAIN WHITE BREAD

PREP TIME: 10 MINUTES
RISING TIME: 1-2 HOURS
BAKING TIME: APPROXIMATELY 1 HOUR
COMPLEXITY: BEGINNER

TOOL FUNCTION:
BREAD MAKER OPERATING SETTING:
BASIC/WHITE BREAD SETTING
BAKING TEMPERATURE: 375°F (190°C)

TOOLS NEEDED:
BREAD MAKER
MEASURING CUPS AND
SPOONS

INGREDIENTS	1 POUND	1.5 POUND	2 POUND
WARM WATER	¾ cup (180 ml)	1 cup (240 ml)	1 ¼ cups (300 ml)
OLIVE OIL	2 tbsp. (30 ml)	3 tbsp. (45 ml)	4 tbsp. (60 ml)
HONEY	2 tbsp. (30 ml)	3 tbsp. (45 ml)	4 tbsp. (60 ml)
SALT	1 tsp. (5 g)	1 ½ tsp. (7.5 g)	2 tsp. (10 g)
WHOLE WHEAT FLOUR	1 cup (120 g)	1 ½ cups (180 g)	2 cups (240 g)
BREAD FLOUR	½ cup (60 g)	¾ cup (90 g)	1 cup (120 g)
SLICED ALMONDS	¼ cup (30 g)	⅓ cup (40 g)	½ cup (60 g)
ACTIVE DRY YEAST	1 ½ tsp. (4.5 g)	2 tsp. (6 g)	2 ½ tsp. (7.5 g)

INSTRUCTIONS

1. Fill the bread maker pan with all the ingredients in the order listed, starting with combining the liquids, followed by the dry ingredients, ensuring the yeast is added last, on top of the flour.
2. Select the Basic/White Bread setting on the bread maker and choose the desired loaf size (1 pound, 1.5 pounds, or 2 pounds).
3. Start the bread maker. The process of mixing the ingredients will begin.
4. Allow the dough to rise in the bread maker for approximately 1 hour or until it reaches the top of the pan.
5. The bread maker will automatically start the baking cycle once the rising cycle is complete.
6. Once the baking cycle is complete, before slicing, cool on a wire rack when it has been removed from the pan.

NUTRITION PER SERVING (1 SLICE): CALORIES 140; PROTEIN 6G; FAT 5G; CARBS 23G; FIBER 4G; SODIUM 180MG

POPPY SEED WHOLE GRAIN WHITE BREAD

PREP TIME: 10 MINUTES
RISING TIME: 1-2 HOURS
BAKING TIME: APPROXIMATELY 1 HOUR
COMPLEXITY: BEGINNER

TOOL FUNCTION:
BREAD MAKER OPERATING SETTING:
BASIC/ WHITE BREAD SETTING
BAKING TEMPERATURE: 375°F (190°C)

TOOLS NEEDED:
BREAD MAKER
MEASURING CUPS AND
SPOONS

INGREDIENTS	1 POUND	1.5 POUND	2 POUND
WARM WATER	¾ cup (180 ml)	1 cup (240 ml)	1 ¼ cups (300 ml)
OLIVE OIL	2 tbsp. (30 ml)	3 tbsp. (45 ml)	4 tbsp. (60 ml)
HONEY	2 tbsp. (30 ml)	3 tbsp. (45 ml)	4 tbsp. (60 ml)
SALT	1 tsp. (5 g)	1 ½ tsp. (7.5 g)	2 tsp. (10 g)
WHOLE WHEAT FLOUR	1 cup (120 g)	1 ½ cups (180 g)	2 cups (240 g)
BREAD FLOUR	½ cup (60 g)	¾ cup (90 g)	1 cup (120 g)
POPPY SEEDS	2 tbsp. (20 g)	3 tbsp. (30 g)	¼ cup (40 g)
ACTIVE DRY YEAST	1 ½ tsp. (4.5 g)	2 tsp. (6 g)	2 ½ tsp. (7.5 g)

INSTRUCTIONS

1. Fill the bread maker pan with all the ingredients in the order listed, starting with combining the liquids, followed by the dry ingredients, ensuring the yeast is added last, on top of the flour.
2. Select the Basic/White Bread setting on the bread maker and choose the desired loaf size (1 pound, 1.5 pounds, or 2 pounds).
3. Start the bread maker. The process of mixing the ingredients will begin.
4. Allow the dough to rise in the bread maker for approximately 1 hour or until it reaches the top of the pan.
5. The bread maker will automatically start the baking cycle once the rising cycle is complete.
6. After the baking cycle, before slicing, cool on a wire rack when it has been removed from the pan.

NUTRITION PER SERVING (1 SLICE): CALORIES 140; PROTEIN 5G; FAT 3G; CARBS 24G; FIBER 4G; SODIUM 180MG

SESAME SEED WHOLE GRAIN WHITE BREAD

PREP TIME: 10 MINUTES
RISING TIME: 1-2 HOURS
BAKING TIME: APPROXIMATELY 1 HOUR
COMPLEXITY: BEGINNER

TOOL FUNCTION:
BREAD MAKER OPERATING SETTING:
BASIC/WHITE BREAD SETTING
BAKING TEMPERATURE: 375°F (190°C)

TOOLS NEEDED:
BREAD MAKER
MEASURING CUPS AND
SPOONS

INGREDIENTS	1 POUND	1.5 POUND	2 POUND
WARM WATER	¾ cup (180 ml)	1 cup (240 ml)	1 ¼ cups (300 ml)
OLIVE OIL	2 tbsp. (30 ml)	3 tbsp. (45 ml)	4 tbsp. (60 ml)
HONEY	2 tbsp. (30 ml)	3 tbsp. (45 ml)	4 tbsp. (60 ml)
SALT	1 tsp. (5 g)	1 ½ tsp. (7.5 g)	2 tsp. (10 g)
WHOLE WHEAT FLOUR	1 cup (120 g)	1 ½ cups (180 g)	2 cups (240 g)
BREAD FLOUR	½ cup (60 g)	¾ cup (90 g)	1 cup (120 g)
SESAME SEEDS	2 tbsp. (20 g)	3 tbsp. (30 g)	¼ cup (40 g)
ACTIVE DRY YEAST	1 ½ tsp. (4.5 g)	2 tsp. (6 g)	2 ½ tsp. (7.5 g)

INSTRUCTIONS

1. Fill the bread machine pan with all the ingredients in the order listed, starting with combining the liquids, followed by the dry ingredients, ensuring the yeast is added last, on top of the flour.
2. Select the Basic/White Bread setting on the bread maker and choose the desired loaf size (1 pound, 1.5 pounds, or 2 pounds).
3. Start the bread maker. The process of mixing the ingredients will begin.
4. Allow the dough to rise in the bread maker for approximately 1 hour or until it reaches the top of the pan.
5. The bread maker will automatically start the baking cycle once the rising cycle is complete.
6. After the baking cycle, before slicing, cool on a wire rack when it has been removed from the pan.

NUTRITION PER SERVING (1 SLICE): CALORIES 140; PROTEIN 5G; FAT 3G; CARBS 24G; FIBER 4G; SODIUM 180MG

WHOLE GRAIN WHITE BREAD WITH MILLET

PREP TIME: 10 MINUTES
RISING TIME: 1-2 HOURS
BAKING TIME: APPROXIMATELY 1 HOUR
COMPLEXITY: BEGINNER

TOOL FUNCTION:
BREAD MAKER OPERATING SETTING:
BASIC/ WHITE BREAD SETTING
BAKING TEMPERATURE: 375°F (190°C)

TOOLS NEEDED:
BREAD MAKER
MEASURING CUPS AND
SPOONS

INGREDIENTS	1 POUND	1.5 POUND	2 POUND
WARM WATER	¾ cup (180 ml)	1 cup (240 ml)	1 ¼ cups (300 ml)
OLIVE OIL	2 tbsp. (30 ml)	3 tbsp. (45 ml)	4 tbsp. (60 ml)
HONEY	2 tbsp. (30 ml)	3 tbsp. (45 ml)	4 tbsp. (60 ml)
SALT	1 tsp. (5 g)	1 ½ tsp. (7.5 g)	2 tsp. (10 g)
WHOLE WHEAT FLOUR	1 cup (120 g)	1 ½ cups (180 g)	2 cups (240 g)
BREAD FLOUR	½ cup (60 g)	¾ cup (90 g)	1 cup (120 g)
MILLET	¼ cup (30 g)	⅓ cup (40 g)	½ cup (60 g)
ACTIVE DRY YEAST	1 ½ tsp. (4.5 g)	2 tsp. (6 g)	2 ½ tsp. (7.5 g)

INSTRUCTIONS

1. Fill the bread maker pan with all the ingredients in the order listed, starting with combining the liquids, followed by the dry ingredients, ensuring the yeast is added last, on top of the flour.
2. Select the Basic/White Bread setting on the bread maker and choose the desired loaf size (1 pound, 1.5 pounds, or 2 pounds).
3. Start the bread maker. The process of mixing the ingredients will begin.
4. Allow the dough to rise in the bread maker for approximately 1 hour or until it reaches the top of the pan.
5. The bread maker will automatically start the baking cycle once the rising cycle is complete.
6. After the baking cycle, before slicing, cool on a wire rack when it has been removed from the pan.

NUTRITION PER SERVING (1 SLICE): CALORIES 140; PROTEIN 5G; FAT 3G; CARBS 24G; FIBER 4G; SODIUM 180MG

WHOLE GRAIN WHITE BREAD WITH AMARANTH

PREP TIME: 10 MINUTES
RISING TIME: 1-2 HOURS
BAKING TIME: APPROXIMATELY 1 HOUR
COMPLEXITY: BEGINNER

TOOL FUNCTION:
BREAD MAKER OPERATING SETTING:
BASIC/WHITE BREAD SETTING
BAKING TEMPERATURE: 375°F (190°C)

TOOLS NEEDED:
BREAD MAKER
MEASURING CUPS AND
SPOONS

INGREDIENTS	1 POUND	1.5 POUND	2 POUND
WARM WATER	¾ cup (180 ml)	1 cup (240 ml)	1 ¼ cups (300 ml)
OLIVE OIL	2 tbsp. (30 ml)	3 tbsp. (45 ml)	4 tbsp. (60 ml)
HONEY	2 tbsp. (30 ml)	3 tbsp. (45 ml)	4 tbsp. (60 ml)
SALT	1 tsp. (5 g)	1 ½ tsp. (7.5 g)	2 tsp. (10 g)
WHOLE WHEAT FLOUR	1 cup (120 g)	1 ½ cups (180 g)	2 cups (240 g)
BREAD FLOUR	½ cup (60 g)	¾ cup (90 g)	1 cup (120 g)
AMARANTH	¼ cup (30 g)	⅓ cup (40 g)	½ cup (60 g)
ACTIVE DRY YEAST	1 ½ tsp. (4.5 g)	2 tsp. (6 g)	2 ½ tsp. (7.5 g)

INSTRUCTIONS

1. Fill the bread maker pan with all the ingredients in the order listed, starting with combining the liquids, followed by the dry ingredients, ensuring the yeast is added last, on top of the flour.
2. Select the Basic/White Bread setting on the bread maker and choose the desired loaf size (1 pound, 1.5 pounds, or 2 pounds).
3. Start the bread maker. The process of mixing the ingredients will begin.
4. Allow the dough to rise in the bread maker for approximately 1 hour or until it reaches the top of the pan.
5. The bread maker will automatically start the baking cycle once the rising cycle is complete.
6. After the baking cycle, before slicing, cool on a wire rack when it has been removed from the pan.

NUTRITION PER SERVING (1 SLICE): CALORIES 140; PROTEIN 5G; FAT 3G; CARBS 24G; FIBER 4G; SODIUM 180MG

QUICK BREAD

PARMESAN-SAGE BEER BREAD

PREP TIME: 10 MINUTES
RISING TIME: 1-2 HOURS
BAKING TIME: APPROXIMATELY 1 HOUR
COMPLEXITY: BEGINNER

TOOL FUNCTION:
BREAD MAKER OPERATING SETTING: QUICK BREAD SETTING
BAKING TEMPERATURE: BREAD MAKER DEFAULT

TOOLS NEEDED:
BREAD MAKER
MEASURING CUPS AND SPOONS

INGREDIENTS	1 POUND	1.5 POUND	2 POUND
ALL-PURPOSE FLOUR	2 ½ cups (295 g)	3 ¾ cups (445 g)	5 cups (590 g)
GRATED PARMESAN CHEESE	1 cup (100 g)	1 ½ cups (150 g)	2 cups (200 g)
SUGAR	2 tbsps. (25 g)	3 tbsps. (35 g)	¼ cup (50 g)
BAKING POWDER	3 tsps. (15 g)	4 ½ tsps. (22.5 g)	2 tbsps. + 2 tsps. (30 g)
FRESH SAGE	1 tbsp. (5 g)	1 ½ tbsps. (7.5 g)	2 ⅔ tbsps. (20 g)
SALT	1 tsp. (5 g)	1 ½ tsps. (7.5 g)	2 tsps. (10 g)
BEER	1 ½ cups (355 ml)	2 ¼ cups (532 ml)	3 cups (710 ml)
MELTED BUTTER	¼ cup (60 ml), divided	⅓ cup (80 ml), divided	½ cup (120 ml), divided

INSTRUCTIONS

1. Lightly grease the bread pan with some of the melted butter.
2. Add the beer, flour, grated Parmesan cheese, sugar, baking powder, chopped fresh sage, and salt in the bread pan.
3. Incorporate the bread pan into the bread machine. Close the lid.
4. Select the "Quick Bread" function.
5. If available, choose your preferred crust darkness.
6. Start the machine to begin mixing and baking.
7. During the baking cycle, open the lid carefully and drizzle the remaining melted butter over the top of the dough.
8. After baking, carefully remove the bread pan from the machine. Give the bread ten minutes or so to cool in the pan.
9. Transfer the bread to a wire rack to cool completely before slicing and serving.

NUTRITION PER SERVING (1 SLICE): CALORIES 150; PROTEIN 3G; FAT 6G; CARBS 21G; FIBER 1G; SODIUM 220MG

EASY QUICK BREAD

PREP TIME: 10 MINUTES BAKING TIME: APPROXIMATELY 1 HOUR COMPLEXITY: BEGINNER	TOOL FUNCTION: BREAD MAKER OPERATING SETTING: QUICK BREAD SETTING BAKING TEMPERATURE: BREAD MAKER DEFAULT		TOOLS NEEDED: BREAD MAKER MEASURING CUPS AND SPOONS

INGREDIENTS	1 POUND	1.5 POUND	2 POUND
ALL-PURPOSE FLOUR	1 cup (120 g)	180 g (1 ½ cups)	2 cups (240 g)
BAKING SODA	1 tsp. (5 g)	1 ½ tsp. (7.5 g)	2 tsp. (10 g)
SALT	½ tsp. (3 g)	¾ tsp. (3.75 g)	½ tsp. (3 g)
GRANULATED SUGAR	½ cup (100 g)	⅜ cup (75 g)	½ cup (100 g)
MILK	½ cup (120 ml)	⅜ cup (90 ml)	½ cup (120 ml)
VEGETABLE OIL	¼ cup (60 ml)	3 tbsp. (45 ml)	¼ cup (60 ml)
EGGS	2	2	2
VANILLA EXTRACT	1 tsp. (5 ml)	1 tsp. (5 ml)	1 tsp. (5 ml)

INSTRUCTIONS
1. Fill the bread machine pan with all the ingredients in the order listed for the desired loaf size.
2. Select the Quick Bread setting on the bread maker.
3. Start the bread maker.
4. Allow the bread maker to run through its cycle, which typically takes about 1 hour.
5. Once the baking cycle is complete, remove the bread from the bread maker and move it to a cooling wire rack.
6. Once cooled, slice the bread and serve.

NUTRITION PER SERVING (1 SLICE): CALORIES 150; PROTEIN 3G; FAT 6G; CARBS 21G; FIBER 1G; SODIUM 220MG

HERB QUICK BREAD

PREP TIME: 10 MINUTES BAKING TIME: APPROXIMATELY 1 HOUR COMPLEXITY: BEGINNER	TOOL FUNCTION: BREAD MAKER OPERATING SETTING: QUICK BREAD SETTING BAKING TEMPERATURE: BREAD MAKER DEFAULT)		TOOLS NEEDED: BREAD MAKER MEASURING CUPS AND SPOONS MIXING BOWL

INGREDIENTS	1 POUND	1.5 POUND	2 POUND
ALL-PURPOSE FLOUR	2 cups (236 g)	3 cups (355 g)	4 cups (473 g)
SUGAR	2 tbsp. + 2 tsp. (25 g)	3 tbsp. + 1 ½ tsp. (37.5 g)	¼ cup + 1 tbsp. + 1 tsp. (50 g)
BAKING POWDER	2 tsp. (8 g)	1 tbsp. + ½ tsp. (12 g)	2 tbsp. (24 g)
CARAWAY SEEDS	2 tsp. (4 g)	1 tbsp. + ½ tsp. (6 g)	2 tbsp. (8 g)
SALT	¼ tsp. (1.5 g)	⅜ tsp. (2.25 g)	½ tsp. (3 g)
GROUND NUTMEG	¼ tsp. (0.6 g)	⅜ tsp. (0.9 g)	½ tsp. (1.2 g)
DRIED THYME	¼ tsp. (0.25 g)	⅜ tsp. (0.375 g)	½ tsp. (0.5 g)
LARGE EGGS	1	1	2
FAT-FREE MILK	½ cup (120 ml)	¾ cup (180 ml)	1 ½ cups (360 ml)
CANOLA OIL	3 tbsp. (40 ml)	¼ cup + 1 tbsp. (60 ml)	⅓ cup (80 ml)

INSTRUCTIONS
1. Grease the bread pan lightly with some oil or butter.
2. Add all-purpose flour, sugar, baking powder, caraway seeds, salt, ground nutmeg, and dried thyme in the bread pan.
3. Crack the egg into another bowl, then lightly beat it. Pour the beaten egg, fat-free milk, and canola oil into the bread pan.
4. Place the bread pan into the bread machine.
5. Select the appropriate setting for a quick bread or cake, typically the "Quick Bread" function, and ensure the stirring function is activated.
6. Start the bread machine to begin the mixing and kneading process. The machine will mix the ingredients thoroughly until forms a smooth dough.
7. The bread machine will proceed with the baking process once the mixing is complete.
8. Allow the bread machine to complete the baking cycle. It usually takes about 1 hour but may vary depending on your machine.
9. After the baking cycle, carefully remove the bread pan from the machine.
10. After a few minutes, first, let the bread to cool within the pan, then remove it to a wire tray to finish cooling.
11. Slice the cooled Herb Quick Bread and serve it as desired.

NUTRITION PER SERVING (1 SLICE): CALORIES 150; PROTEIN 3G; FAT 6G; CARBS 21G; FIBER 1G; SODIUM 220MG

CHOCOLATE QUICK BREAD

PREP TIME: 10 MINUTES
BAKING TIME: APPROXIMATELY 1 HOUR
COMPLEXITY: BEGINNER

TOOL FUNCTION:
BREAD MAKER OPERATING SETTING: QUICK BREAD SETTING
BAKING TEMPERATURE: BREAD MAKER DEFAULT

TOOLS NEEDED:
BREAD MAKER
MEASURING CUPS AND SPOONS
MIXING BOWL

INGREDIENTS	1 POUND	1.5 POUND	2 POUND
ALL-PURPOSE FLOUR	1 ¾ cups (207.5 g)	2-⅝ cups (311.25 g)	3 ½ cups (415 g)
BAKING COCOA	½ cup (50 g)	¾ cup (75 g)	1 cup (100 g)
BAKING POWDER	½ tsp. (2.5 g)	¾ tsp. (3.75 g)	1 tsp. (5 g)
BAKING SODA	½ tsp. (2.5 g)	¾ tsp. (3.75 g)	1 tsp. (5 g)
SALT	½ tsp. (3 g)	¾ tsp. (4.5 g)	1 tsp. (6 g)
BUTTER	½ cup (113 g)	¾ cup (170 g)	1 cup (226 g)
SUGAR	1 cup (200 g)	1 ½ cups (300 g)	2 cups (400 g)
EGGS	2 large	3 large	4 large
BUTTERMILK	1 cup (240 ml)	1 ½ cups (360 ml)	2 cups (480 ml)
MINI CHOCOLATE CHIPS	½ cup (85 g)	¾ cup (127.5 g)	1 cup (170 g)
CHOPPED PECANS	⅓ cup (40 g)	½ cup (60 g)	⅔ cup (80 g)

INSTRUCTIONS

1. Add the salt, all-purpose flour, baking soda, baking powder, and baking cocoa in the bread pan.
2. Cream the sugar and softened butter in a separate bowl until light and fluffy.
3. Beat thoroughly after adding each egg to the buttersugar mixture. Add the eggs one at a time.
4. Stir in the buttermilk until well combined.
5. Pour the wet ingredients into the bread pan with the dry ingredients.
6. Add the miniature semisweet chocolate chips and chopped pecans to the bread pan.
7. In the bread machine, place the bread pan.
8. Choose the appropriate setting for a quick bread or cake, typically the "Quick Bread" function, and ensure that the stirring function is activated.
9. Start the bread machine to begin the mixing and baking process. The machine will mix the ingredients thoroughly until a smooth batter forms and then proceed with the baking process.
10. Allow the bread machine to complete the baking cycle. It usually takes about 1 hour but may vary depending on your machine.
11. After the baking cycle, carefully remove the bread pan from the machine.
12. Before moving the chocolate quick bread to a wire rack to cool completely, let it cool in the pan for a few minutes.
13. Slice the cooled Chocolate Quick Bread and serve it as desired.

NUTRITION PER SERVING (1 SLICE): : CALORIES 150; PROTEIN 3G; FAT 6G; CARBS 21G; FIBER 1G; SODIUM 220MG

COCONUT QUICK BREAD

PREP TIME: 10 MINUTES
BAKING TIME: APPROXIMATELY 1 HOUR
COMPLEXITY: BEGINNER

TOOL FUNCTION:
BREAD MAKER OPERATING SETTING:
QUICK BREAD SETTING
BAKING TEMPERATURE: BREAD MAKER
DEFAULT

TOOLS NEEDED:
BREAD MAKER
MEASURING CUPS AND
SPOONS
KNIFE AND CUTTING BOARD

INGREDIENTS	1 POUND	1.5 POUND	2 POUND
ALL-PURPOSE FLOUR	1 cup (120 g)	1 ½ cups (180 g)	2 cups (240 g)
BAKING SODA	½ tsp. (3 g)	¾ tsp. (3.75 g)	1 tsp. (5 g)
SALT	¼ tsp. (1.5 g)	⅜ tsp. (2.25 g)	½ tsp. (3 g)
GRANULATED SUGAR	¼ cup (50 g)	⅜ cup (75 g)	½ cup (100 g)
COCONUT MILK	¼ cup (60 ml)	⅜ cup (90 ml)	½ cup (120 ml)
VEGETABLE OIL	⅛ cup (30 ml)	3 tbsps. (45 ml)	¼ cup (60 ml)
EGG	1	1	2
VANILLA EXTRACT	½ tsp. (2.5 ml)	¾ tsp. (3.75 ml)	1 tsp. (5 ml)
SHREDDED COCONUT	¼ cup (20 g)	⅜ cup (30 g)	½ cup (40 g)

INSTRUCTIONS

1. Fill the bread machine pan with all the ingredients in the order listed for the desired loaf size.
2. Select the Quick Bread setting on the bread maker.
3. Start the bread maker.
4. Allow the bread maker to run through its cycle, which typically takes about 1 hour.
5. Once the baking cycle is complete, remove the bread from the bread maker and move it to a cooling wire rack.
6. Once cooled, slice the bread and serve.

NUTRITION PER SERVING (1 SLICE): CALORIES 180; PROTEIN 3G; FAT 8G; CARBS 23G; FIBER 1G; SODIUM 230MG

STRAWBERRY QUICK BREAD

PREP TIME: 10 MINUTES
BAKING TIME: APPROXIMATELY 1 HOUR
COMPLEXITY: BEGINNER

TOOL FUNCTION:
BREAD MAKER OPERATING SETTING:
QUICK BREAD SETTING
BAKING TEMPERATURE: BREAD MAKER
DEFAULT

TOOLS NEEDED:
BREAD MAKER
MEASURING CUPS AND
SPOONS
KNIFE AND CUTTING BOARD

INGREDIENTS	1 POUND	1.5 POUND	2 POUND
ALL-PURPOSE FLOUR	1 cup (120 g)	1 ½ cups (180 g)	2 cups (240 g)
BAKING SODA	½ tsp. (3 g)	¾ tsp. (3.75 g)	1 tsp. (5 g)
SALT	¼ tsp. (1.5 g)	⅜ tsp. (2.25 g)	½ tsp. (3 g)
GRANULATED SUGAR	¼ cup (50 g)	⅜ cup (75 g)	½ cup (100 g)
MILK	½ cup (120 ml)	⅜ cup (90 ml)	½ cup (120 ml)
VEGETABLE OIL	¼ cup (60 ml)	3 tbsps. (45 ml)	¼ cup (60 ml)
EGGS	2	1	2
VANILLA EXTRACT	½ tsp. (2.5 ml)	¾ tsp. (3.75 ml)	1 tsp. (5 ml)
CHOPPED STRAWBERRIES	½ cup (75 g)	¾ cup (110 g)	1 cup (150 g)

INSTRUCTIONS

1. Fill the bread machine pan with all the ingredients in the order listed for the desired loaf size.
2. Select the Quick Bread setting on the bread maker.
3. Start the bread maker.
4. Allow the bread maker to run through its cycle, which typically takes about 1 hour.
5. Once the baking cycle is complete, remove the bread from the bread maker and move it to a cooling wire rack.
6. Once cooled, slice the bread and serve.

NUTRITION PER SERVING (1 SLICE): CALORIES 170; PROTEIN 3G; FAT 7G; CARBS 23G; FIBER 1G; SODIUM 230MG

ORANGE QUICK BREAD

PREP TIME: 10 MINUTES
BAKING TIME: APPROXIMATELY 1 HOUR
COMPLEXITY: BEGINNER

TOOL FUNCTION:
BREAD MAKER OPERATING SETTING: QUICK
BREAD SETTING
BAKING TEMPERATURE: BREAD MAKER
DEFAULT

TOOLS NEEDED:
BREAD MAKER
MEASURING CUPS AND SPOONS

INGREDIENTS	1 POUND	1.5 POUND	2 POUND
ALL-PURPOSE FLOUR	1 cup (120 g)	1 ½ cups (180 g)	2 cups (240 g)
BAKING SODA	½ tsp. (3 g)	¾ tsp. (3.75 g)	1 tsp. (5 g)
SALT	¼ tsp. (1.5 g)	⅜ tsp. (2.25 g)	½ tsp. (3 g)
GRANULATED SUGAR	¼ cup (50 g)	⅜ cup (75 g)	½ cup (100 g)
MILK	½ cup (120 ml)	⅜ cup (90 ml)	½ cup (120 ml)
VEGETABLE OIL	¼ cup (60 ml)	3 tbsps. (45 ml)	¼ cup (60 ml)
EGGS	2	1	2
ORANGE (JUICE & ZEST)	Juice and zest of ½ orange	Juice and zest of 1 orange	Juice and zest of 1 orange

INSTRUCTIONS

1. Fill the bread machine pan with all the ingredients in the order listed for the desired loaf size.
2. Select the Quick Bread setting on the bread maker.
3. Start the bread maker.
4. Allow the bread maker to run through its cycle, which typically takes about 1 hour.
5. Once the baking cycle is complete, remove the bread from the bread maker and move it to a cooling wire rack.
6. Once cooled, slice the bread and serve.

NUTRITION PER SERVING (1 SLICE): CALORIES 160; PROTEIN 3G; FAT 6G; CARBS 23G; FIBER 1G; SODIUM 230MG

VINEGAR AND LEMON QUICK BREAD

PREP TIME: 10 MINUTES
BAKING TIME: APPROXIMATELY 1 HOUR
COMPLEXITY: BEGINNER

TOOL FUNCTION:
BREAD MAKER OPERATING SETTING:
QUICK BREAD SETTING
BAKING TEMPERATURE: BREAD MAKER
DEFAULT

TOOLS NEEDED:
BREAD MAKER
MEASURING CUPS AND SPOONS

INGREDIENTS	1 POUND	1.5 POUND	2 POUND
ALL-PURPOSE FLOUR	1 cup (120 g)	1 ½ cups (180 g)	2 cups (240 g)
BAKING SODA	½ tsp. (3 g)	¾ tsp. (3.75 g)	1 tsp. (5 g)
SALT	¼ tsp. (1.5 g)	⅜ tsp. (2.25 g)	½ tsp. (3 g)
GRANULATED SUGAR	¼ cup (50 g)	⅜ cup (75 g)	½ cup (100 g)
VINEGAR	½ tbsp. (7.5 ml)	¾ tbsp. (11.25 ml)	1 tbsp. (15 ml)
MILK	½ cup (120 ml)	¾ cup (180 ml)	1 cup (240 ml)
VEGETABLE OIL	¼ cup (60 ml)	3 tbsps. (45 ml)	¼ cup (60 ml)
EGGS	2	1	2
LEMON JUICE & ZEST	1 lemon	1 lemon	1 lemon

INSTRUCTIONS

1. Fill the bread machine pan with all the ingredients in the order listed for the desired loaf size.
2. Select the Quick Bread setting on the bread maker.
3. Start the bread maker.
4. Allow the bread maker to run through its cycle, which typically takes about 1 hour.
5. Once the baking cycle is complete, remove the bread from the bread maker and move it to a cooling wire rack.
6. Once cooled, slice the bread and serve.

NUTRITION PER SERVING (1 SLICE): CALORIES 160; PROTEIN 3G; FAT 7G; CARBS 21G; FIBER 1G; SODIUM 240MG

SOURDOUGH BREAD

CLASSIC SOURDOUGH BREAD

PREP TIME: 15 MINUTES
RISE TIME: 24 HOURS (OVERNIGHT)
BAKING TIME: 40-45 MINUTES
COMPLEXITY: INTERMEDIATE

TOOL FUNCTION:
BREAD MAKER OPERATING
SETTING: BASIC/WHITE BREAD
SETTING
BAKING TEMPERATURE: 375°F (190°C)

TOOLS NEEDED:
BREAD MAKER
MEASURING CUPS AND SPOONS
MEDIUM-SIZED GLASS OR PLASTIC
CONTAINER

INGREDIENTS	SOURDOUGH STARTER	1 POUND	1.5 POUND	2 POUND
ALL-PURPOSE FLOUR	1 cup (120 g)			
WARM WATER	½ cup (120 ml)	½ cup + 2 tbsp. (150 ml)	¾ cup + 1 tbsp. (195 ml)	1 cup + 3 tbsp. (240 ml)
BREAD FLOUR		1 cup + 2 tbsp. (150 g)	1 ½ cups + 1 tbsp. (225 g)	2 cups + 3 tbsp. (300 g)
SALT		½ tsp. (3 g)	¾ tsp. (4.5 g)	1 tsp. (6 g)

INSTRUCTIONS

Making the Sourdough Starter:

1. Combine the flour and warm water in a medium-sized glass or plastic container.
2. Mix thoroughly to ensure no dry spots and the mixture is well combined.
3. Cover the container using a fresh cloth or plastic wrap, fastening it with an elastic band or tape to allow air circulation.
4. Place the container in a warm area, ideally around 75-80°F (24-27°C), for 24 hours.
5. After 24 hours, check the starter. It should appear bubbly and have a slightly tangy aroma. If not, let it ferment at room temperature for another 12-24 hours until it becomes active.
6. Once the starter is active, it can be used in the Whole wheat Sourdough Bread recipe

Making the Bread:

1. Combine the warm water and sourdough starter in the bread machine pan.
2. Add the bread flour and salt to the liquid mixture, ensuring it covers the liquid completely.
3. Place the bread machine pan into the bread machine and select the desired loaf size (1 pound, 1.5 pounds, or 2 pounds).
4. Select the Basic or White Bread setting on the bread machine.
5. Start the bread machine and let it run through its cycle, including mixing, kneading, rising, and baking.
6. Once the baking cycle is complete, take caution when taking the bread out of the bread maker. To allow the pan to cool down before slicing, place it on a wire rack.

- -

NUTRITION PER SERVING (1 SLICE): CALORIES 120; PROTEIN 3G; FAT 0.5G; CARBS 25G; FIBER 1G; SODIUM 250MG

WHOLE WHEAT SOURDOUGH BREAD

PREP TIME: 15 MINUTES
RISE TIME: 24 HOURS (OVERNIGHT)
BAKING TIME: 40-45 MINUTES
COMPLEXITY: INTERMEDIATE

TOOL FUNCTION:
BREAD MAKER OPERATING SETTING:
WHOLE WHEAT SETTING
BAKING TEMPERATURE: 375°F (190°C)

TOOLS NEEDED:
BREAD MAKER
MEASURING CUPS AND SPOONS
MEDIUM-SIZED GLASS OR
PLASTIC CONTAINER

INGREDIENTS	SOURDOUGH STARTER	1 POUND	1.5 POUND	2 POUND
ALL-PURPOSE FLOUR	1 cup (120 g)			
WARM WATER	½ cup (120 ml)	½ cup + 2 tbsp. (150 ml)	¾ cup + 1 tbsp. (195 ml)	1 cup + 3 tbsp. (240 ml)
WHOLE WHEAT FLOUR		1½ cups + 1 tbsp. (180 g)	2¼ cups (270 g)	3 cups (360 g)
BREAD FLOUR		½ cup (60 g)	¾ cup (90 g)	1 cup (120 g)
SALT		1 tsp. (6 g)	¾ tsp. (4.5 g)	1 tsp. (6 g)

INSTRUCTIONS

Making the Sourdough Starter:
1. Combine the whole wheat flour and warm water in a medium-sized glass or plastic container.
2. Mix thoroughly to ensure no dry spots and the mixture is well combined.
3. Cover the container using a fresh cloth or plastic wrap, fastening it with an elastic band or tape to allow air circulation.
4. Place the container in a warm area, ideally around 75-80°F (24-27°C), for 24 hours.
5. After 24 hours, check the starter. It should appear bubbly and have a slightly tangy aroma. If not, let it ferment at room temperature for another 12-24 hours until it becomes active.
6. Once the starter is active, it can be used in the Whole wheat Sourdough Bread recipe.

Making the Bread:
1. Combine the warm water and sourdough starter in the bread machine pan.
2. Add the whole wheat flour, bread flour, and salt to the liquid mixture, ensuring it covers the liquid completely.
3. Place the bread machine pan into the bread machine and select the desired loaf size (1 pound, 1.5 pounds, or 2 pounds).
4. Start the bread machine and let it run through its cycle, including mixing, kneading, rising, and baking.
5. Once the baking cycle is complete, take caution when taking the bread out of the bread maker. To allow the pan to cool down before slicing, place it on a wire rack.

NUTRITION PER SERVING (1 SLICE): CALORIES 125; PROTEIN 3G; FAT 0.5G; CARBS 28G; FIBER 4G; SODIUM 250MG

RYE SOURDOUGH BREAD

PREP TIME: 15 MINUTES
RISE TIME: 24 HOURS (OVERNIGHT)
BAKING TIME: 40-45 MINUTES
COMPLEXITY: INTERMEDIATE

TOOL FUNCTION:
BREAD MAKER OPERATING SETTING:
WHOLE WHEAT SETTING
BAKING TEMPERATURE: 375°F (190°C)

TOOLS NEEDED:
BREAD MAKER
MEASURING CUPS AND SPOONS
MEDIUM-SIZED GLASS OR PLASTIC
CONTAINER

INGREDIENTS	SOURDOUGH STARTER	1 POUND	1.5 POUND	2 POUND
RYE FLOUR	1 cup (120 g)	1 ½ cups (180 g)	2 ¼ cups (270 g)	3 cups (360 g)
WARM WATER	½ cup (120 ml)	½ cup + 2 tbsp. (150 ml)	¾ cup + 1 tbsp. (195 ml)	1 cup + 3 tbsp. (240 ml)
BREAD FLOUR		½ cup (60 g)	¾ cup (90 g)	1 cup (120 g)
SALT		1 tsp. (6 g)	¾ tsp. (4.5 g)	1 tsp. (6 g)

INSTRUCTIONS

Making the Sourdough Starter:
1. Combine the rye flour and warm water in a medium-sized glass or plastic container.
2. Mix thoroughly to ensure no dry spots and the mixture is well combined.
3. Cover the container using a fresh cloth or plastic wrap, fastening it with an elastic band or tape to allow air circulation.
4. Place the container in a warm area, ideally around 75-80°F (24-27°C), for 24 hours.
5. After 24 hours, check the starter. It should appear bubbly and have a slightly tangy aroma. If not, let it ferment at room temperature for another 12-24 hours until it becomes active.
6. Once the starter is active, it can be used in the Rye Sourdough Bread recipe.

Making the Bread:
1. Combine the warm water and sourdough starter in the bread machine pan.
2. Add the whole wheat flour, bread flour, and salt to the liquid mixture, ensuring it covers the liquid completely.
3. Place the bread machine pan into the bread machine and select the desired loaf size (1 pound, 1.5 pounds, or 2 pounds).
4. Start the bread machine and let it run through its cycle, including mixing, kneading, rising, and baking.
5. Once the baking cycle is complete, take caution when taking the bread out of the bread maker pan and allow it to cool on a cooling rack prior to slicing.

NUTRITION PER SERVING (1 SLICE): CALORIES 120; PROTEIN 5G; FAT 1G; CARBS 25G; FIBER 3G; SODIUM 250MG

KAMUT SOURDOUGH BREAD

PREP TIME: 15 MINUTES
RISE TIME: 24 HOURS (OVERNIGHT)
BAKING TIME: 40-45 MINUTES
COMPLEXITY: INTERMEDIATE

TOOL FUNCTION:
BREAD MAKER OPERATING SETTING:
WHOLE WHEAT SETTING
BAKING TEMPERATURE: 375°F (190°C)

TOOLS NEEDED:
BREAD MAKER
MEASURING CUPS AND SPOONS
MEDIUM-SIZED GLASS OR
PLASTIC CONTAINER

INGREDIENTS	SOURDOUGH STARTER	1 POUND	1.5 POUND	2 POUND
KAMUT FLOUR	1 cup (120 g)	1 ½ cups (180 g)	2 ¼ cups (270 g)	3 cups (360 g)
WARM WATER	½ cup (120 ml)	½ cup + 2 tbsp. (150 ml)	¾ cup + 1 tbsp. (195 ml)	1 cup + 3 tbsp. (240 ml)
BREAD FLOUR		½ cup (60 g)	¾ cup (90 g)	1 cup (120 g)
SALT		1 tsp. (6 g)	¾ tsp. (4.5 g)	1 tsp. (6 g)

INSTRUCTIONS

Making the Sourdough Starter:

1. In a medium-sized glass or plastic container, combine the kamut flour and warm water.
2. Mix thoroughly to ensure no dry spots and the mixture is well combined.
3. Cover the container using a fresh cloth or plastic wrap, fastening it with an elastic band or tape to allow air circulation.
4. Place the container in a warm area, ideally around 75-80°F (24-27°C), for 24 hours.
5. After 24 hours, check the starter. It should appear bubbly and have a slightly tangy aroma. If not, let it ferment at room temperature for another 12-24 hours until it becomes active.
6. Once the starter is active, it is ready for use in the Kamut Sourdough Bread recipe.

Making the Bread:

1. Combine the warm water and kamut sourdough starter in the bread machine pan.
2. Add the kamut flour, bread flour, and salt to the liquid mixture, ensuring it covers the liquid completely.
3. Place the bread machine pan into the bread machine and select the desired loaf size (1 pound, 1.5 pounds, or 2 pounds).
4. Start the bread machine and let it run through its cycle, including mixing, kneading, rising, and baking.
5. Once the baking cycle is complete, take caution when taking the bread out of the bread maker. To allow the pan to cool down before slicing, place it on a wire rack.

NUTRITION PER SERVING (1 SLICE): CALORIES 110; PROTEIN 3G; FAT 0,5G; CARBS 22G; FIBER 3G; SODIUM 200MG

BUCKWHEAT SOURDOUGH BREAD

PREP TIME: 15 MINUTES
RISE TIME: 24 HOURS (OVERNIGHT)
BAKING TIME: 40-45 MINUTES
COMPLEXITY: INTERMEDIATE

TOOL FUNCTION:
BREAD MAKER OPERATING SETTING: WHOLE WHEAT SETTING
BAKING TEMPERATURE: 375°F (190°C)

TOOLS NEEDED:
BREAD MAKER
MEASURING CUPS AND SPOONS
MEDIUM-SIZED GLASS OR PLASTIC CONTAINER

INGREDIENTS	SOURDOUGH STARTER	1 POUND	1.5 POUND	2 POUND
BUCKWHEAT FLOUR	1 cup (120 g)	1 ½ cups (180 g)	2 ¼ cups (270 g)	3 cups (360 g)
WARM WATER	½ cup (120 ml)	½ cup + 2 tbsp. (150 ml)	¾ cup + 1 tbsp. (195 ml)	1 cup + 3 tbsp. (240 ml)
BREAD FLOUR		½ cup (60 g)	¾ cup (90 g)	1 cup (120 g)
SALT		1 tsp. (6 g)	¾ tsp. (4.5 g)	1 tsp. (6 g)

INSTRUCTIONS

Making the Sourdough Starter:

1. Combine the buckwheat flour and warm water in a medium-sized glass or plastic container.
2. Mix thoroughly to ensure no dry spots and the mixture is well combined.
3. Cover the container using a fresh cloth or plastic wrap, fastening it with an elastic band or tape to allow air circulation.
4. Place the container in a warm area, ideally around 75-80°F (24-27°C), for 24 hours.
5. After 24 hours, check the starter. It should appear bubbly and have a slightly tangy aroma. If not, let it ferment at room temperature for another 12-24 hours until it becomes active.
6. Once the starter is active, it can be used in the Buckwheat Sourdough Bread recipe.

Making the Bread:

1. Combine the warm water and buckwheat sourdough starter in the bread machine pan.
2. Add the buckwheat flour, bread flour, and salt to the liquid mixture, ensuring it covers the liquid completely.
3. Place the bread machine pan into the bread machine and select the desired loaf size (1 pound, 1.5 pounds, or 2 pounds).
4. Start the bread machine and let it run through its cycle, including mixing, kneading, rising, and baking.
5. Once the baking cycle is complete, take caution when taking the bread out of the bread maker. To allow the pan to cool down before slicing, place it on a wire rack.

NUTRITION PER SERVING (1 SLICE): CALORIES 110; PROTEIN 3G; FAT 0,5G; CARBS 22G; FIBER 3G; SODIUM 200MG

BARLEY SOURDOUGH BREAD

PREP TIME: 15 MINUTES
RISE TIME: 24 HOURS (OVERNIGHT)
BAKING TIME: 40-45 MINUTES
COMPLEXITY: INTERMEDIATE

TOOL FUNCTION:
BREAD MAKER OPERATING SETTING: WHOLE WHEAT SETTING
BAKING TEMPERATURE: 375°F (190°C)

TOOLS NEEDED:
BREAD MAKER
MEASURING CUPS AND SPOONS
MEDIUM-SIZED GLASS OR PLASTIC CONTAINER

INGREDIENTS	SOURDOUGH STARTER	1 POUND	1.5 POUND	2 POUND
BARLEY FLOUR	1 cup (120 g)	1 ½ cups (180 g)	2 ¼ cups (270 g)	3 cups (360 g)
WARM WATER	½ cup (120 ml)	½ cup + 2 tbsp. (150 ml)	¾ cup + 1 tbsp. (195 ml)	1 cup + 3 tbsp. (240 ml)
BREAD FLOUR		½ cup (60 g)	¾ cup (90 g)	1 cup (120 g)
SALT		1 tsp. (6 g)	¾ tsp. (4.5 g)	1 tsp. (6 g)

INSTRUCTIONS

Making the Sourdough Starter:

1. Combine the barley flour and warm water in a medium-sized glass or plastic container.
2. Mix thoroughly to ensure no dry spots and the mixture is well combined.
3. Cover the container using a fresh cloth or plastic wrap, fastening it with an elastic band or tape to allow air circulation.
4. Place the container in a warm area, ideally around 75-80°F (24-27°C), for 24 hours.
5. After 24 hours, check the starter. It should appear bubbly and have a slightly tangy aroma. If not, let it ferment at room temperature for another 12-24 hours until it becomes active.
6. Once the starter is active, it can be used in the Barley Sourdough Bread recipe.

Making the Bread:

1. Combine the warm water and barley sourdough starter in the bread machine pan.
2. Add the barley flour, bread flour, and salt to the liquid mixture, ensuring it covers the liquid completely.
3. Place the bread machine pan into the bread machine and select the desired loaf size (1 pound, 1.5 pounds, or 2 pounds).
4. Start the bread machine and let it run through its cycle, including mixing, kneading, rising, and baking.
5. Once the baking cycle is complete, take caution when taking the bread out of the bread maker. To allow the pan to cool down before slicing, place it on a wire rack.

NUTRITION PER SERVING (1 SLICE): CALORIES 125; PROTEIN 5G; FAT 0,5G; CARBS 24G; FIBER 1G; SODIUM 200MG

OAT SOURDOUGH BREAD

PREP TIME: 15 MINUTES
RISE TIME: 24 HOURS (OVERNIGHT)
BAKING TIME: 40-45 MINUTES
COMPLEXITY: INTERMEDIATE

TOOL FUNCTION:
BREAD MAKER OPERATING SETTING:
WHOLE WHEAT SETTING
BAKING TEMPERATURE: 375°F (190°C)

TOOLS NEEDED:
BREAD MAKER
MEASURING CUPS AND SPOONS
MEDIUM-SIZED GLASS OR PLASTIC CONTAINER

INGREDIENTS	SOURDOUGH STARTER	1 POUND	1.5 POUND	2 POUND
OAT FLOUR	1 cup (120 g)	1 ½ cups (180 g)	2 ¼ cups (270 g)	3 cups (360 g)
WARM WATER	½ cup (120 ml)	½ cup + 2 tbsp. (150 ml)	¾ cup + 1 tbsp. (195 ml)	1 cup + 3 tbsp. (240 ml)
BREAD FLOUR		½ cup (60 g)	¾ cup (90 g)	1 cup (120 g)
SALT		1 tsp. (6 g)	¾ tsp. (4.5 g)	1 tsp. (6 g)

INSTRUCTIONS

Making the Sourdough Starter:

1. Combine the oat flour and warm water in a medium-sized glass or plastic container.
2. Mix thoroughly to ensure no dry spots and the mixture is well combined.
3. Cover the container using a fresh cloth or plastic wrap, fastening it with an elastic band or tape to allow air circulation.
4. Place the container in a warm area, ideally around 75-80°F (24-27°C), for 24 hours.
5. After 24 hours, check the starter. It should appear bubbly and have a slightly tangy aroma. If not, let it ferment at room temperature for another 12-24 hours until it becomes active.
6. Once the starter is active, it is ready for use in the Oat Sourdough Bread recipe.

Making the Bread:

1. Combine the warm water and oat sourdough starter in the bread machine pan.
2. Add the oat flour, bread flour, and salt to the liquid mixture, ensuring it covers the liquid completely.
3. Place the bread machine pan into the bread machine and select the desired loaf size (1 pound, 1.5 pounds, or 2 pounds).
4. Start the bread machine and let it run through its cycle, including mixing, kneading, rising, and baking.
5. Once the baking cycle is complete, take caution when taking the bread out of the bread maker. To allow the pan to cool down before slicing, place it on a wire rack.

- -

NUTRITION PER SERVING (1 SLICE): CALORIES 110; PROTEIN 3G; FAT 0,5G; CARBS 22G; FIBER 1G; SODIUM 200MG

SORGHUM SOURDOUGH BREAD

PREP TIME: 15 MINUTES
RISE TIME: 24 HOURS (OVERNIGHT)
BAKING TIME: 40-45 MINUTES
COMPLEXITY: INTERMEDIATE

TOOL FUNCTION:
BREAD MAKER OPERATING SETTING: WHOLE
WHEAT SETTING
BAKING TEMPERATURE: 375°F (190°C)

TOOLS NEEDED:
BREAD MAKER
MEASURING CUPS AND SPOONS
MEDIUM-SIZED GLASS OR PLASTIC
CONTAINER

INGREDIENTS	SOURDOUGH STARTER	1 POUND	1.5 POUND	2 POUND
SORGHUM FLOUR	1 cup (120 g)	1 ½ cups (180 g)	2 ¼ cups (270 g)	3 cups (360 g)
WARM WATER	½ cup (120 ml)	½ cup + 2 tbsp. (150 ml)	¾ cup + 1 tbsp. (195 ml)	1 cup + 3 tbsp. (240 ml)
BREAD FLOUR		½ cup (60 g)	¾ cup (90 g)	1 cup (120 g)
SALT		1 tsp. (6 g)	¾ tsp. (4.5 g)	1 tsp. (6 g)

INSTRUCTIONS

Making the Sourdough Starter:

1. Combine the sorghum flour and warm water in a medium-sized glass or plastic container.
2. Mix thoroughly to ensure no dry spots and the mixture is well combined.
3. Cover the container using a fresh cloth or plastic wrap, fastening it with an elastic band or tape to allow air circulation.
4. Place the container in a warm area, ideally around 75-80°F (24-27°C), for 24 hours.
5. After 24 hours, check the starter. It should appear bubbly and have a slightly tangy aroma. If not, let it ferment at room temperature for another 12-24 hours until it becomes active.
6. Once the starter is active, it can be used in the Sorghum Sourdough Bread recipe.

Making the Bread:

1. Combine the warm water and sorghum sourdough starter in the bread machine pan.
2. Add the sorghum flour, bread flour, and salt to the liquid mixture, ensuring it covers the liquid completely.
3. Place the bread machine pan into the bread machine and select the desired loaf size (1 pound, 1.5 pounds, or 2 pounds).
4. Start the bread machine and let it run through its cycle, including mixing, kneading, rising, and baking.
5. Once the baking cycle is complete, take caution when taking the bread out of the bread maker. To allow the pan to cool down before slicing, place it on a wire rack.

- -

NUTRITION PER SERVING (1 SLICE): CALORIES 115; PROTEIN 3G; FAT 0,5G; CARBS 24G; FIBER 2G; SODIUM 200MG

TEFF SOURDOUGH BREAD

PREP TIME: 15 MINUTES
RISE TIME: 24 HOURS (OVERNIGHT)
BAKING TIME: 40-45 MINUTES
COMPLEXITY: INTERMEDIATE

TOOL FUNCTION:
BREAD MAKER OPERATING SETTING:
WHOLE WHEAT SETTING
BAKING TEMPERATURE: 375°F (190°C)

TOOLS NEEDED:
BREAD MAKER
MEASURING CUPS AND SPOONS
MEDIUM-SIZED GLASS OR PLASTIC CONTAINER

INGREDIENTS	SOURDOUGH STARTER	1 POUND	1.5 POUND	2 POUND
TEFF FLOUR	1 cup (120 g)	1 ½ cups (180 g)	2 ¼ cups (270 g)	3 cups (360 g)
WARM WATER	½ cup (120 ml)	½ cup + 2 tbsp. (150 ml)	¾ cup + 1 tbsp. (195 ml)	1 cup + 3 tbsp. (240 ml)
BREAD FLOUR		½ cup (60 g)	¾ cup (90 g)	1 cup (120 g)
SALT		1 tsp. (6 g)	¾ tsp. (4.5 g)	1 tsp. (6 g)

INSTRUCTIONS

Making the Sourdough Starter:

1. Combine the teff flour and warm water in a medium-sized glass or plastic container.
2. Mix thoroughly to ensure no dry spots and the mixture is well combined.
3. Cover the container using a fresh cloth or plastic wrap, fastening it with an elastic band or tape to allow air circulation.
4. Place the container in a warm area, ideally around 75-80°F (24-27°C), for 24 hours.
5. After 24 hours, check the starter. It should appear bubbly and have a slightly tangy aroma. If not, let it ferment at room temperature for another 12-24 hours until it becomes active.
6. Once the starter is active, it can be used in the Teff Sourdough Bread recipe.

Making the Bread:

1. Combine the warm water and teff sourdough starter in the bread machine pan.
2. Add the teff flour, bread flour, and salt to the liquid mixture, ensuring it covers the liquid completely.
3. Place the bread machine pan into the bread machine and select the desired loaf size (1 pound, 1.5 pounds, or 2 pounds).
4. Start the bread machine and let it run through its cycle, including mixing, kneading, rising, and baking.
5. Once the baking cycle is complete, take caution when taking the bread out of the bread maker. To allow the pan to cool down before slicing, place it on a wire rack.

NUTRITION PER SERVING (1 SLICE): CALORIES 110; PROTEIN 3G; FAT 0,5G; CARBS 22G; FIBER 2G; SODIUM 200MG

MULTIGRAIN SOURDOUGH BREAD

PREP TIME: 15 MINUTES
RISE TIME: 24 HOURS (OVERNIGHT)
BAKING TIME: 40-45 MINUTES
COMPLEXITY: INTERMEDIATE

TOOL FUNCTION:
BREAD MAKER OPERATING SETTING:
WHOLE WHEAT SETTING
BAKING TEMPERATURE: 375°F (190°C)

TOOLS NEEDED:
BREAD MAKER
MEASURING CUPS AND SPOONS
MEDIUM-SIZED GLASS OR PLASTIC CONTAINER

INGREDIENTS	SOURDOUGH STARTER	1 POUND	1.5 POUND	2 POUND
WHOLE WHEAT FLOUR	1 cup (120 g)	½ cup (60 g)	¾ cup (90 g)	1 cup (120 g)
WARM WATER	½ cup (120 ml)	½ cup + 2 tbsp. (150 ml)	¾ cup + 1 tbsp. (195 ml)	1 cup + 3 tbsp. (240 ml)
RYE FLOUR		½ cup (60 g)	¾ cup (90 g)	1 cup (120 g)
SPELT FLOUR		½ cup (60 g)	¾ cup (90 g)	1 cup (120 g)
BREAD FLOUR		½ cup (60 g)	¾ cup (90 g)	1 cup (120 g)
SALT		1 tsp. (6 g)	¾ tsp. (4.5 g)	1 tsp. (6 g)

INSTRUCTIONS

Making the Sourdough Starter:

1. Combine the whole flour and warm water in a medium-sized glass or plastic container.
2. Mix thoroughly to ensure no dry spots and the mixture is well combined.
3. Cover the container using a fresh cloth or plastic wrap, fastening it with an elastic band or tape to allow air circulation.
4. Place the container in a warm area, ideally around 75-80°F (24-27°C), for 24 hours.
5. After 24 hours, check the starter. It should appear bubbly and have a slightly tangy aroma. If not, let it ferment at room temperature for another 12-24 hours until it becomes active.
6. Once the starter is active, it is ready for use in the Multigrain Sourdough Bread recipe.

Making the Bread:

1. Combine the warm water and multigrain sourdough starter in the bread machine pan.
2. Add the whole wheat flour, rye flour, spelt flour, bread flour, and salt on top of the liquid mixture, ensuring it covers the liquid completely.
3. Place the bread machine pan into the bread machine and select the desired loaf size (1 pound, 1.5 pounds, or 2 pounds).
4. Start the bread machine and let it run through its cycle, including mixing, kneading, rising, and cooking.
5. After the baking cycle is over, take the bread out with caution from the bread machine. To allow the pan to cool down before slicing, place it on a wire rack.

NUTRITION PER SERVING (1 SLICE): CALORIES 110; PROTEIN 3G; FAT 0,5G; CARBS 22G; FIBER 3G; SODIUM 200MG

BUCKWHEAT AND ALMOND SOURDOUGH BREAD

PREP TIME: 15 MINUTES
RISE TIME: 24 HOURS (OVERNIGHT)
BAKING TIME: 40-45 MINUTES
COMPLEXITY: INTERMEDIATE

TOOL FUNCTION:
BREAD MAKER OPERATING SETTING:
WHOLE WHEAT SETTING
BAKING TEMPERATURE: 375°F (190°C)

TOOLS NEEDED:
BREAD MAKER
MEASURING CUPS AND SPOONS
MEDIUM-SIZED GLASS OR PLASTIC CONTAINER

INGREDIENTS	SOURDOUGH STARTER	1 POUND	1.5 POUND	2 POUND
BUCKWHEAT FLOUR	1 cup (120 g)	1 ¼ cups + 1 tbsp. (150 g)	1 ⅞ cups (225 g)	2 ½ cups (300 g)
WARM WATER	½ cup (120 ml)	½ cup + 2 tbsp. (150 ml)	¾ cup + 1 tbsp. (195 ml)	1 cup + 3 tbsp. (240 ml)
ALMOND FLOUR		¼ cup (30 g)	⅜ cup (45 g)	½ cup (60 g)
BREAD FLOUR		½ cup (60 g)	¾ cup (90 g)	1 cup (120 g)
SALT		1 tsp. (6 g)	¾ tsp. (4.5 g)	1 tsp. (6 g)

INSTRUCTIONS

Making the Sourdough Starter:

1. Combine the buckwheat flour and warm water in a medium-sized glass or plastic container.
2. Mix thoroughly to ensure no dry spots and the mixture is well combined.
3. Cover the container using a fresh cloth or plastic wrap, fastening it with an elastic band or tape to allow air circulation.
4. Place the container in a warm area, ideally around 75-80°F (24-27°C), for 24 hours.
5. After 24 hours, check the starter. It should appear bubbly and have a slightly tangy aroma. If not, let it ferment at room temperature for another 12-24 hours until it becomes active.
6. Once the starter is active, it can be used in the Buckwheat Sourdough Bread recipe.

Making the Bread:

1. Combine the warm water and buckwheat sourdough starter in the bread machine pan.
2. Add the buckwheat flour, almond flour, bread flour, and salt on top of the liquid mixture, ensuring it covers the liquid completely.
3. Place the bread machine pan into the bread machine and select the desired loaf size (1 pound, 1.5 pounds, or 2 pounds).
4. Start the bread machine and let it run through its cycle, including mixing, kneading, rising, and baking.
5. Once the baking cycle is complete, take caution when taking the bread out of the bread maker. To allow the pan to cool down before slicing, place it on a wire rack.

- -

NUTRITION PER SERVING (1 SLICE): CALORIES 110; PROTEIN 3G; FAT 0,5G; CARBS 22G; FIBER 2G; SODIUM 200MG

QUINOA SOURDOUGH BREAD

PREP TIME: 15 MINUTES
RISE TIME: 24 HOURS (OVERNIGHT)
BAKING TIME: 40-45 MINUTES
COMPLEXITY: INTERMEDIATE

TOOL FUNCTION:
BREAD MAKER OPERATING SETTING:
WHOLE WHEAT SETTING
BAKING TEMPERATURE: 375°F (190°C)

TOOLS NEEDED:
BREAD MAKER
MEASURING CUPS AND SPOONS
MEDIUM-SIZED GLASS OR PLASTIC CONTAINER

INGREDIENTS	SOURDOUGH STARTER	1 POUND	1.5 POUND	2 POUND
QUINOA FLOUR	1 cup (120 g)	1 ½ cups + 1 tbsp. (180 g)	2 ¼ cups (270 g)	3 cups (360 g)
WARM WATER	½ cup (120 ml)	½ cup + 2 tbsp. (150 ml)	¾ cup + 1 tbsp. (195 ml)	1 cup + 3 tbsp. (240 ml)
BREAD FLOUR		½ cup (60 g)	¾ cup (90 g)	1 cup (120 g)
SALT		1 tsp. (6 g)	¾ tsp. (4.5 g)	1 tsp. (6 g)

INSTRUCTIONS

Making the Sourdough Starter:

1. Combine the quinoa flour and warm water in a medium-sized glass or plastic container.
2. Mix thoroughly to ensure no dry spots and the mixture is well combined.
3. Cover the container using a fresh cloth or plastic wrap, fastening it with an elastic band or tape to allow air circulation.
4. Place the container in a warm area, ideally around 75-80°F (24-27°C), for 24 hours.
5. After 24 hours, check the starter. It should appear bubbly and have a slightly tangy aroma. If not, let it ferment at room temperature for another 12-24 hours until it becomes active.
6. Once the starter is active, it is ready for use in the Quinoa Sourdough Bread recipe.

Making the Bread:

1. Combine the warm water and quinoa sourdough starter in the bread machine pan.
2. Add the quinoa flour, bread flour, and salt to the liquid mixture, ensuring it covers the liquid completely.
3. Place the bread machine pan into the bread machine and select the desired loaf size (1 pound, 1.5 pounds, or 2 pounds).
4. Start the bread machine and let it run through its cycle, including mixing, kneading, rising, and baking.
5. Once the baking cycle is complete, take caution when taking the bread out of the bread maker. To allow the pan to cool down before slicing, place it on a wire rack.

- -

NUTRITION PER SERVING (1 SLICE): CALORIES 110; PROTEIN 3G; FAT 0,5G; CARBS 22G; FIBER 2G; SODIUM 200MG

GLUTEN-FREE BREAD

CLASSIC GLUTEN-FREE WHITE BREAD

PREP TIME: 10 MINUTES
RISING TIME: 1-2 HOURS
BAKING TIME: APPROXIMATELY 1 HOUR
COMPLEXITY: BEGINNER

TOOL FUNCTION:
BREAD MAKER OPERATING SETTING:
GLUTEN-FREE SETTING
BAKING TEMPERATURE: 375°F (190°C)

TOOLS NEEDED:
BREAD MAKER
MEASURING CUPS AND SPOONS

INGREDIENTS	1 POUND	1.5 POUND	2 POUND
GLUTEN-FREE ALL-PURPOSE FLOUR BLEND	1 cup (120 g)	180 g (1 ½ cups)	2 cups (240 g)
BAKING SODA	½ tsp. (3 g)	¾ tsp. (4.5 g)	1 tsp. (5 g)
SALT	¼ tsp. (1.5 g)	⅜ tsp. (2.25 g)	½ tsp. (3 g)
GRANULATED SUGAR	¼ cup (50 g)	⅜ cup (75 g)	½ cup (100 g)
VINEGAR	½ tbsp. (7.5 ml)	¾ tbsp. (11.25 ml)	1 tbsp. (15 ml)
MILK	½ cup (120 ml)	¾ cup (180 ml)	1 cup (240 ml)
VEGETABLE OIL	¼ cup (60 ml)	3 tbsp. (45 ml)	¼ cup (60 ml)
EGGS	2	1	2
VANILLA EXTRACT	½ tsp. (2.5 ml)	¾ tsp. (3.75 ml)	1 tsp. (5 ml)

INSTRUCTIONS

1. Fill the bread machine pan with all the ingredients in the order listed, starting with combining the liquids, followed by the dry ingredients, ensuring the yeast is added last, on top of the flour.
2. Select the Gluten-Free setting on the bread maker and choose the desired loaf size (1 pound, 1.5 pounds, or 2 pounds).
3. Start the bread maker. The process of mixing the ingredients will begin.
4. Let the dough rise in the bread maker for approximately 1 hour or until it reaches the top of the pan.
5. The bread maker will automatically start the baking cycle once the rising cycle is complete.
6. After the baking cycle, before slicing, cool on a wire rack when it has been removed from the pan.

NUTRITION PER SERVING (1 SLICE): CALORIES 120; PROTEIN 2G; FAT 5G; CARBS 18G; FIBER 1G; SODIUM 180MG

GLUTEN-FREE SEEDED BREAD

PREP TIME: 15 MINUTES
RISING TIME: 1-2 HOURS
BAKING TIME: APPROXIMATELY 1 HOUR
COMPLEXITY: BEGINNER

TOOL FUNCTION:
BREAD MAKER OPERATING SETTING:
GLUTENFREE SETTING
BAKING TEMPERATURE: 375°F (190°C)

TOOLS NEEDED:
BREAD MAKER
MEASURING CUPS AND SPOONS

INGREDIENTS	1 POUND	1.5 POUND	2 POUND
HONEY	1 tbsp. (20 g)	1 ½ tbsps. (30 g)	2 tbsps. (40 g)
LARGE EGG	1	1	2
VEGETABLE OIL	2 tbsps. (30 ml)	3 tbsps. (45 ml)	¼ cup (60 ml)
WARM WATER	½ cup (120 ml)	¾ cup (180 ml)	1 cup (240 ml)
MIXED SEEDS (Sunflower, Pumpkin, Sesame, Flax)	2 tbsps. (15 g)	3 tbsps. (22.5 g)	¼ cup (30 g)
GLUTEN-FREE ALL-PURPOSE FLOUR BLEND	1 cup (140 g)	1 ½ cups (210 g)	2 cups (280 g)
TAPIOCA FLOUR	2 tbsps. (30 g)	3 tbsps. (45 g)	¼ cup (60 g)
POTATO STARCH	2 tbsps. (30 g)	3 tbsps. (45 g)	¼ cup (60 g)
GROUND CHIA SEEDS	¾ tsp. (about 4 g)	¾ tsp. (about 4 g)	1 tsp. (about 5 g)
ACTIVE DRY YEAST	1 tsp. (4 g)	1 ½ tsps. (6 g)	1 tbsp. (12 g)
SALT	½ tsp. (3 g)	¾ tsp. (5 g)	1 tsp. (5 g)

INSTRUCTIONS

1. Fill the bread maker with all the ingredients pan in the order listed, starting with combining the liquids, followed by the dry ingredients, ensuring the yeast is added last, on top of the flour.
2. Select the Gluten-Free setting on the bread maker and choose the desired loaf size (1 pound, 1.5 pounds, or 2 pounds).
3. Start the bread maker. The process of mixing the ingredients will begin.
4. Let the dough rise in the bread maker for approximately 1 hour or until it reaches the top of the pan.
5. The bread maker will automatically start the baking cycle once the rising cycle is complete.
6. After the baking cycle, before slicing, cool on a wire rack when it has been removed from the pan.

NUTRITION PER SERVING (1 SLICE): CALORIES 160; PROTEIN 4G; FAT 8G; CARBS 20G; FIBER 2G; SODIUM 160MG

GLUTEN-FREE NUTTY BREAD

PREP TIME: 15 MINUTES
RISING TIME: 1-2 HOURS
BAKING TIME: APPROXIMATELY 1 HOUR
COMPLEXITY: BEGINNER

TOOL FUNCTION:
BREAD MAKER OPERATING SETTING:
GLUTENFREE SETTING
BAKING TEMPERATURE: 375°F (190°C)

TOOLS NEEDED:
BREAD MAKER
MEASURING CUPS AND SPOONS
KNIFE AND CUTTING BOARD

INGREDIENTS	1 POUND	1.5 POUND	2 POUND
HONEY	1 tbsp. (20 g)	1 ½ tbsps. (30 g)	2 tbsps. (40 g)
LARGE EGG	1	1	2
VEGETABLE OIL	2 tbsps. (30 ml)	3 tbsps. (45 ml)	¼ cup (60 ml)
WARM WATER	½ cup (120 ml)	¾ cup (180 ml)	1 cup (240 ml)
GLUTEN-FREE ALL-PURPOSE FLOUR BLEND	1 cup (140 g)	1 ½ cups (210 g)	2 ¼ cups (315 g)
ALMOND FLOUR	⅓ cup (47 g)	½ cup (70 g)	¾ cup (105 g)
TAPIOCA FLOUR	2 tbsps. (30 g)	3 tbsps. (45 g)	¼ cup (60 g)
POTATO STARCH	2 tbsps. (30 g)	3 tbsps. (45 g)	¼ cup (60 g)
XANTHAN GUM	1 tsp. (5.3 g)	1 ½ tsps. (8 g)	2 tsps. (10 g)
ACTIVE DRY YEAST	1 tsp. (4 g)	1 ½ tsps. (6 g)	2 tsps. (8 g)
SALT	½ tsp. (3 g)	¾ tsp. (5 g)	1 ½ tsps. (9 g)
CHOPPED NUTS (Almonds, Walnuts, Pecans)	¼ cup (30 g)	⅓ cup (40 g)	½ cup (60 g)

INSTRUCTIONS

1. Fill the bread maker pan with all the ingredients in the order listed, starting with combining the liquids, followed by the dry ingredients, ensuring the yeast is added last, on top of the flour.
2. Select the Gluten-Free setting on the bread maker and choose the desired loaf size (1 pound, 1.5 pounds, or 2 pounds).
3. Start the bread maker. The process of mixing the ingredients will begin.
4. Let the dough rise in the bread maker for approximately 1 hour or until it reaches the top of the pan.
5. The bread maker will automatically start the baking cycle once the rising cycle is complete.
6. After the baking cycle, before slicing, cool on a wire rack when it has been removed from the pan.

GLUTEN-FREE BANANA BREAD

PREP TIME: 15 MINUTES
RISING TIME: 1-2 HOURS
BAKING TIME: APPROXIMATELY 1 HOUR
COMPLEXITY: INTERMEDIATE

TOOL FUNCTION:
BREAD MAKER OPERATING
SETTING: GLUTENFREE SETTING
BAKING TEMPERATURE: 375°F
(190°C)

TOOLS NEEDED:
BREAD MAKER
MEASURING CUPS AND SPOONS
MIXING BOWL
KNIFE AND CUTTING BOARD

INGREDIENTS	1 POUND	1.5 POUND	2 POUND
GLUTEN-FREE ALL-PURPOSE FLOUR BLEND	1 cup (140 g)	1 ½ cups (210 g)	2 cups (280 g)
TAPIOCA FLOUR	2 tbsps. (30 g)	3 tbsps. (45 g)	¼ cup (60 g)
POTATO STARCH	2 tbsps. (30 g)	3 tbsps. (45 g)	¼ cup (60 g)
XANTHAN GUM	1 tsp. (5.3 g)	1 ½ tsps. (8 g)	1 ½ tsps. (8 g)
ACTIVE DRY YEAST	½ tsp. (3 g)	¾ tsp. (4 g)	1 tsp. (5 g)
SALT	½ tsp. (3 g)	¾ tsp. (5 g)	1 tsp. (6 g)
SUGAR	¼ cup (50 g)	⅓ cup (70 g)	½ cup (100 g)
VEGETABLE OIL	2 tbsps. (30 ml)	3 tbsps. (45 ml)	¼ cup (60 ml)
LARGE EGG	1	1	2
MASHED RIPE BANANAS	½ cup (120 ml)	¾ cup (180 ml)	1 cup (240 ml)
VANILLA EXTRACT	½ tsp. (2.5 ml)	¾ tsp. (3.75 ml)	1 tsp. (5 ml)

INSTRUCTIONS

1. Combine the gluten-free all-purpose flour blend, tapioca flour, potato starch, xanthan gum, yeast, salt, and sugar in a mixing bowl. Thoroughly stir to guarantee that all components are dispersed equally.
2. Combine the vegetable oil, eggs, mashed bananas, and vanilla extract and whisk in another basin until smooth.
3. The wet ingredients should be stirred into the dry ingredients gradually and continuously until forms a smooth batter.
4. Lightly grease the bread maker pan with oil or nonstick cooking spray.
5. Pour the batter into the bread maker pan, distributing it evenly to guarantee a consistent loaf.
6. Place the bread maker pan into the bread maker and select the desired loaf size (one pound, one and a half, or two pounds) and additionally the Gluten-Free setting. Set the baking temperature to 375°F (190°C).
7. Start the bread maker and allow it to run through its cycle, including mixing, kneading, rising, and baking. The rising time may vary depending on room temperature and humidity, but it typically takes 60-90 minutes.
8. Once the baking cycle is complete, carefully remove the bread from the bread maker. To allow the pan to cool down before slicing, place it on a wire rack.

GLUTEN-FREE LEMON POPPY SEED BREAD

PREP TIME: 15 MINUTES
RISING TIME: 1-2 HOURS
BAKING TIME: APPROXIMATELY 1 HOUR
COMPLEXITY: BEGINNER

TOOL FUNCTION:
BREAD MAKER OPERATING SETTING:
GLUTENFREE SETTING
BAKING TEMPERATURE: 375°F (190°C)

TOOLS NEEDED:
BREAD MAKER
MEASURING CUPS AND SPOONS

INGREDIENTS	1 POUND	1.5 POUND	2 POUND
VEGETABLE OIL	2 tbsps. (30 ml)	3 tbsps. (45 ml)	¼ cup (60 ml)
LARGE EGG	1	1	2
LEMON JUICE	2 tbsps. (30 ml)	3 tbsps. (45 ml)	¼ cup (60 ml)
LEMON ZEST	Zest of 1 lemon	Zest of 1 lemon	Zest of 1 lemon
GLUTEN-FREE ALL-PURPOSE FLOUR BLEND	1 cup + 2 tbsps. (140 g)	1 ½ cups (210 g)	2 cups + 4 tbsps. (280 g)
TAPIOCA FLOUR	2 tbsps. (30 g)	3 tbsps. (45 g)	¼ cup (60 g)
POTATO STARCH	2 tbsps. (30 g)	3 tbsps. (45 g)	¼ cup (60 g)
XANTHAN GUM	1 ½ tsps. (6 g)	1 ½ tsps. (8 g)	2 tsps. (10 g)
ACTIVE DRY YEAST	1 ½ tsps. (8 g)	2 tsps. (8 g)	1 tbsp. (12 g)
SALT	½ tsp. (3 g)	¾ tsp. (4.5 g)	1 tsp. (5 g)
SUGAR	¼ cup (60 g)	⅓ cup (80 g)	½ cup (120 g)
POPPY SEEDS	½ tbsp. (7.5 ml)	¾ tbsp. (11.25 ml)	1 tbsp. (15 ml)

INSTRUCTIONS

1. Fill the bread machine pan with all the ingredients in the order listed, starting with combining the liquids, followed by the dry ingredients, ensuring the yeast is added last, on top of the flour.
2. Select the Gluten-Free setting on the bread maker and choose the desired loaf size (1 pound, 1.5 pounds, or 2 pounds).
3. Start the bread maker. The process of mixing the ingredients will begin.
4. Let the dough rise in the bread maker for approximately 1 hour or until it reaches the top of the pan.
5. The bread maker will automatically start the baking cycle once the rising cycle is complete.
6. After the baking cycle, before slicing, cool on a wire rack when it has been removed from the pan.

- -

NUTRITION PER SERVING (1 SLICE): CALORIES 150; PROTEIN 3G; FAT 6G; CARBS 21G; FIBER 1G; SODIUM 180MG

GLUTEN-FREE CRANBERRY ORANGE BREAD

PREP TIME: 15 MINUTES
RISING TIME: 1-2 HOURS
BAKING TIME: APPROXIMATELY 1 HOUR
COMPLEXITY: BEGINNER

TOOL FUNCTION:
BREAD MAKER OPERATING SETTING:
GLUTENFREE SETTING
BAKING TEMPERATURE: 375°F (190°C)

TOOLS NEEDED:
BREAD MAKER
MEASURING CUPS AND SPOONS
MIXING BOWL

INGREDIENTS	1 POUND	1.5 POUND	2 POUND
VEGETABLE OIL	2 tbsps. (30 ml)	3 tbsps. (45 ml)	¼ cup (60 ml)
LARGE EGGS	2	2	3
ORANGE JUICE	¼ cup (60 ml)	⅓ cup (80 ml)	½ cup (120 ml)
ORANGE ZEST	Zest of 1 orange	Zest of 1 orange	Zest of 1 orange
GLUTEN-FREE ALL-PURPOSE FLOUR BLEND	1 cup + 2 tbsps. (140 g)	1 ½ cups (210 g)	2 cups + 4 tbsps. (280 g)
TAPIOCA FLOUR	2 tbsps. (30 g)	3 tbsps. (45 g)	¼ cup (60 g)
POTATO STARCH	2 tbsps. (30 g)	3 tbsps. (45 g)	¼ cup (60 g)
XANTHAN GUM	1 ½ tsps. (6 g)	1 ½ tsps. (8 g)	2 tsps. (10 g)
ACTIVE DRY YEAST	1 ½ tsps. (6 g)	1 ½ tsps. (8 g)	2 tsps. (10 g)
SALT	½ tsp. (3 g)	¾ tsp. (4.5 g)	1 tsp. (5 g)
SUGAR	¼ cup (60 g)	⅓ cup (80 g)	½ cup (120 g)
DRIED CRANBERRIES	¼ cup (30 g)	⅓ cup (40 g)	½ cup (60 g)

INSTRUCTIONS

1. Fill the bread machine pan with all the ingredients in the order listed, starting with combining the liquids, followed by the dry ingredients, ensuring the yeast is added last, on top of the flour.
2. Select the Gluten-Free setting on the bread maker and choose the desired loaf size (1 pound, 1.5 pounds, or 2 pounds).
3. Start the bread maker. The process of mixing the ingredients will begin.
4. Let the dough rise in the bread maker for approximately 1 hour or until it reaches the top of the pan.
5. The bread maker will automatically start the baking cycle once the rising cycle is complete.
6. After the baking cycle, before slicing, cool on a wire rack when it has been removed from the pan.

- -

NUTRITION PER SERVING (1 SLICE): CALORIES 160; PROTEIN 2G; FAT 6G; CARBS 25G; FIBER 1G; SODIUM 200MG

GLUTEN-FREE CHOCOLATE CHIP BREAD

PREP TIME: 15 MINUTES
RISING TIME: 1-2 HOURS
BAKING TIME: APPROXIMATELY 1 HOUR
COMPLEXITY: BEGINNER

TOOL FUNCTION:
BREAD MAKER OPERATING SETTING:
GLUTENFREE SETTING
BAKING TEMPERATURE: 375°F (190°C)

TOOLS NEEDED:
BREAD MAKER
MEASURING CUPS AND SPOONS

INGREDIENTS	1 POUND	1.5 POUND	2 POUND
VEGETABLE OIL	2 tbsps. (30 ml)	3 tbsps. (45 ml)	¼ cup (60 ml)
LARGE EGGS	2	2	3
VANILLA EXTRACT	1 tsp. (5 ml)	1 ½ tsps. (7.5 ml)	2 tsps. (10 ml)
GLUTEN-FREE ALL-PURPOSE FLOUR BLEND	1 cup + 2 tbsps. (140 g)	1 ½ cups (210 g)	2 cups + 4 tbsps. (280 g)
TAPIOCA FLOUR	2 tbsps. (30 g)	3 tbsps. (45 g)	¼ cup (60 g)
POTATO STARCH	2 tbsps. (30 g)	3 tbsps. (45 g)	¼ cup (60 g)
GROUND CHIA SEEDS	¾ tsp. (about 4 g)	¾ tsp. (about 4 g)	1 tsp. (about 5 g)
ACTIVE DRY YEAST	1 ½ tsps. (6 g)	1 ½ tsps. (8 g)	2 tsps. (10 g)
SALT	½ tsp. (3 g)	¾ tsp. (4.5 g)	1 tsp. (5 g)
SUGAR	¼ cup (60 g)	⅓ cup (80 g)	½ cup (120 g)
GLUTEN-FREE CHOCOLATE CHIPS	¼ cup (45 g)	⅓ cup (60 g)	½ cup (90 g)

INSTRUCTIONS

1. Fill the bread machine pan with all the ingredients in the order listed, starting with combining the liquids, followed by the dry ingredients, ensuring the yeast is added last, on top of the flour.
2. Select the Gluten-Free setting on the bread maker and choose the desired loaf size (1 pound, 1.5 pounds, or 2 pounds).
3. Start the bread maker. The process of mixing the ingredients will begin.
4. Let the dough rise in the bread maker for approximately 1 hour or until it reaches the top of the pan.
5. Bread maker will automatically start the baking cycle once the rising cycle is complete.
6. After the baking cycle, before slicing, cool on a wire rack when it has been removed from the pan.

NUTRITION PER SERVING (1 SLICE): CALORIES 180; PROTEIN 2G; FAT 2G; CARBS 27G; FIBER 1G; SODIUM 200MG

GLUTEN-FREE CARROT BREAD

PREP TIME: 15 MINUTES
RISING TIME: 1-2 HOURS
BAKING TIME: APPROXIMATELY 1 HOUR
COMPLEXITY: BEGINNER

TOOL FUNCTION:
BREAD MAKER OPERATING SETTING:
GLUTENFREE SETTING
BAKING TEMPERATURE: 375°F (190°C)

TOOLS NEEDED:
BREAD MAKER
MEASURING CUPS AND SPOONS
VEGETABLE GRATER

INGREDIENTS	1 POUND	1.5 POUND	2 POUND
GLUTEN-FREE ALL-PURPOSE FLOUR BLEND	1 cup + 2 tbsps. (140 g)	1 ½ cups (210 g)	2 cups + 4 tbsps. (280 g)
TAPIOCA FLOUR	2 tbsps. (30 g)	3 tbsps. (45 g)	¼ cup (60 g)
POTATO STARCH	2 tbsps. (30 g)	3 tbsps. (45 g)	¼ cup (60 g)
GROUND CHIA SEEDS	¾ tsp. (about 4 g)	¾ tsp. (about 4 g)	1 tsp. (about 5 g)
ACTIVE DRY YEAST	1 ½ tsps. (6 g)	1 ½ tsps. (8 g)	2 tsps. (10 g)
SALT	½ tsp. (3 g)	¾ tsp. (4.5 g)	1 tsp. (5 g)
SUGAR	¼ cup (60 g)	⅓ cup (80 g)	½ cup (120 g)
VEGETABLE OIL	2 tbsps. (30 ml)	3 tbsps. (45 ml)	¼ cup (60 ml)
LARGE EGGS	2	2	3
GRATED CARROTS	1 cup (240 ml)	1 ½ cups (360 ml)	2 cups (480 ml)
CHOPPED WALNUTS OR PECANS	¼ cup (30 g)	⅓ cup (40 g)	½ cup (60 g)

INSTRUCTIONS

1. Within the bread machine's pan, combine the gluten-free all-purpose flour blend, tapioca flour, potato starch, ground chia seeds, active dry yeast, salt, and sugar. Make sure the dry ingredients are properly combined by giving them a good stir.
2. Add the vegetable oil, eggs, grated carrots, and chopped walnuts or pecans directly into the bread machine pan on top of the dry ingredients.
3. Place the bread machine pan into the bread machine, select the desired loaf size (one pound, one and a half, or two pounds) and additionally choose the Gluten-Free setting.
4. Start the bread machine and let it run its cycle. It will mix, knead, rise, and bake the bread for you.
5. Once the baking cycle is complete, carefully remove the bread from the machine. Put on a wire rack to cool while it is still in the pan before slicing and serving.

NUTRITION PER SERVING (1 SLICE): CALORIES 180; PROTEIN 3G; FAT 8G; CARBS 24G; FIBER 2G; SODIUM 200MG

GLUTEN-FREE CINNAMON RAISIN BREAD

PREP TIME: 15 MINUTES
RISING TIME: 1-2 HOURS
BAKING TIME: APPROXIMATELY 1 HOUR
COMPLEXITY: BEGINNER

TOOL FUNCTION:
BREAD MAKER OPERATING SETTING:
GLUTENFREE SETTING
BAKING TEMPERATURE: 375°F (190°C)

TOOLS NEEDED:
BREAD MAKER
MEASURING CUPS AND SPOONS

INGREDIENTS	1 POUND	1.5 POUND	2 POUND
WARM WATER	¾ cup (180 ml)	1 cup (240 ml)	1 ¼ cups (300 ml)
VEGETABLE OIL	2 tbsps. (30 ml)	3 tbsps. (45 ml)	¼ cup (60 ml)
LARGE EGG	1	1	2
VANILLA EXTRACT	½ tsp. (2.5 ml)	¾ tsp. (3.7 ml)	1 tsp. (5 ml)
GLUTEN-FREE ALL-PURPOSE FLOUR BLEND	1 cup + 2 tbsps. (150 g)	1 ½ cups (210 g)	2 cups + 4 tbsps. (300 g)
TAPIOCA FLOUR	2 tbsps. (30 g)	3 tbsps. (45 g)	¼ cup (60 g)
POTATO STARCH	2 tbsps. (30 g)	3 tbsps. (45 g)	¼ cup (60 g)
GROUND FLAXSEED MEAL	1 ½ tsps. (4 g)	2 tsps. (5 g)	1 tbsp. (8 g)
ACTIVE DRY YEAST	1 ½ tsps. (8 g)	1 ½ tsps. (8 g)	2 tsps. (10 g)
SALT	½ tsp. (3 g)	¾ tsp. (4.5 g)	1 tsp. (5 g)
SUGAR	¼ cup (60 g)	⅓ cup (80 g)	½ cup (120 g)
RAISINS	½ cup (75 g)	¾ cup (115 g)	1 cup (150 g)
GROUND CINNAMON	1 ½ tsps. (7.5 g)	2 tsps. (10 g)	1 tbsp. (15 g)

INSTRUCTIONS

1. Fill the bread maker pan with all the ingredients in the order listed, starting with combining the liquids, followed by the dry ingredients, ensuring the yeast is added last, on top of the flour.
2. Select the Gluten-Free setting on the bread maker and choose the desired loaf size (1 pound, 1.5 pounds, or 2 pounds).
3. Start the bread maker. The process of mixing the ingredients will begin.
4. Let the dough rise in the bread maker for approximately 1 hour or until it reaches the top of the pan.
5. The bread maker will automatically start the baking cycle once the rising cycle is complete.
6. After the baking cycle, before slicing, cool on a wire rack when it has been removed from the pan.

NUTRITION PER SERVING (1 SLICE): CALORIES 150; PROTEIN 2G; FAT 6G; CARBS 22G; FIBER 1G; SODIUM 150MG

GLUTEN-FREE SUNFLOWER SEED BREAD

PREP TIME: 15 MINUTES
RISING TIME: 1-2 HOURS
BAKING TIME: APPROXIMATELY 1 HOUR
COMPLEXITY: BEGINNER

TOOL FUNCTION:
BREAD MAKER OPERATING SETTING:
GLUTENFREE SETTING
BAKING TEMPERATURE: 375°F (190°C)

TOOLS NEEDED:
BREAD MAKER
MEASURING CUPS AND SPOONS

INGREDIENTS	1 POUND	1.5 POUND	2 POUND
GLUTEN-FREE ALL-PURPOSE FLOUR BLEND	1 cup (140 g)	1 ½ cups (210 g)	2 cups (280 g)
TAPIOCA FLOUR	2 tbsps. (30 g)	3 tbsps. (45 g)	¼ cup (60 g)
POTATO STARCH	2 tbsps. (30 g)	3 tbsps. (45 g)	¼ cup (60 g)
GROUND FLAXSEED MEAL	1 ½ tsps. (4 g)	2 tsps. (5 g)	1 tbsp. (8 g)
ACTIVE DRY YEAST	1 ½ tsps. (6 g)	2 tsps. (8 g)	1 tbsp. (12 g)
SALT	½ tsp. (3 g)	¾ tsp. (4.5 g)	1 tsp. (5 g)
OLIVE OIL	2 tbsps. (30 ml)	3 tbsps. (45 ml)	¼ cup (60 ml)
HONEY	1 tbsp. (15 ml)	1 ½ tbsps. (22.5 ml)	2 tbsps. (30 ml)
LARGE EGG	1	1	2
SUNFLOWER SEEDS	¼ cup (35 g)	⅓ cup (45 g)	½ cup (70 g)

INSTRUCTIONS

1. Fill the bread machine pan with all the ingredients in the order listed, starting with combining the liquids, followed by the dry ingredients, ensuring the yeast is added last, on top of the flour.
2. Select the Gluten-Free setting on the bread maker and choose the desired loaf size (1 pound, 1.5 pounds, or 2 pounds).
3. Start the bread maker. The process of mixing the ingredients will begin.
4. Let the dough rise in the bread maker for approximately 1 hour or until it reaches the top of the pan.
5. The bread maker will automatically start the baking cycle once the rising cycle is complete.
6. Once the baking cycle is complete, before slicing, cool on a wire rack when it has been removed from the pan.

NUTRITION PER SERVING (1 SLICE): CALORIES 150; PROTEIN 4G; FAT 8G; CARBS 15G; FIBER 1G; SODIUM 180MG

MULTIGRAIN BREAD

CLASSIC MULTIGRAIN BREAD

PREP TIME: 15 MINUTES
RISING TIME: 1-2 HOURS
BAKING TIME: APPROXIMATELY 1 HOUR
COMPLEXITY: BEGINNER

TOOL FUNCTION:
BREAD MAKER OPERATING SETTING:
WHOLE WHEAT SETTING
BAKING TEMPERATURE: 375°F (190°C)

TOOLS NEEDED:
BREAD MAKER
MEASURING CUPS AND SPOONS
MIXING BOWL

INGREDIENTS	1 POUND	1.5 POUND	2 POUND
WHOLE WHEAT FLOUR	¾ cup (90 g)	1 ⅛ cups (135 g)	1 ½ cups (180 g)
BREAD FLOUR	¾ cup (90 g)	1 ⅛ cups (135 g)	1 ½ cups (180 g)
ROLLED OATS	¼ cup (30 g)	⅜ cup (45 g)	½ cup (60 g)
WHEAT GERM	2 tbsps. (15 g)	2 tbsps. (30 g)	2 tbsps. (30 g)
FLAXSEEDS	2 tbsps. (15 g)	2 tbsps. (30 g)	2 tbsps. (30 g)
SUNFLOWER SEEDS	2 tbsps. (15 g)	2 tbsps. (30 g)	2 tbsps. (30 g)
SESAME SEEDS	2 tbsps. (15 g)	2 tbsps. (30 g)	2 tbsps. (30 g)
ACTIVE DRY YEAST	½ packet (3.5 g)	¾ packet (5.25 g)	1 packet (7 g)
WARM WATER	¾ cup (180 ml)	1 cup (240 ml)	1 ¼ cups (300 ml)
HONEY	1 tbsp. (15 ml)	1 ½ tbsps. (22.5 ml)	2 tbsps. (30 ml)
OLIVE OIL	1 tbsp. (15 ml)	1 ½ tbsps. (22.5 ml)	2 tbsps. (30 ml)
SALT	½ tsp. (3 g)	¾ tsp. (4.5 g)	1 tsp. (5 g)

INSTRUCTIONS

1. In the bread machine pan, combine the whole wheat flour, bread flour, rolled oats, wheat germ, flaxseeds, sunflower seeds, sesame seeds, and active dry yeast. Perform a thorough mixing to guarantee that the dry ingredients are distributed evenly.
2. Combine the warm water, honey, olive oil, and salt in another bowl until the honey is fully dissolved.
3. Pour the wet ingredients into the bread machine pan over the dry ingredients.
4. Place the bread machine pan into the bread machine and select the desired loaf size (one pound, one and a half, or two pounds) and additionally the whole wheat setting.
5. Start the bread machine and let it run through its cycle, including mixing, kneading, rising, and baking.
6. Once the baking cycle is complete, before slicing, carefully remove the bread from the bread machine pan and allow it to cool on a wire rack.

NUTRITION PER SERVING (1 SLICE): CALORIES 120; PROTEIN 4G; FAT 4G; CARBS 18G; FIBER 3G; SODIUM 150MG

SEEDED MULTIGRAIN BREAD

PREP TIME: 15 MINUTES
RISING TIME: 1-2 HOURS
BAKING TIME: APPROXIMATELY 1 HOUR
COMPLEXITY: BEGINNER

TOOL FUNCTION:
BREAD MAKER OPERATING SETTING:
WHOLE WHEAT SETTING
BAKING TEMPERATURE: 375°F (190°C)

TOOLS NEEDED:
BREAD MAKER
MEASURING CUPS AND SPOONS
MIXING BOWL

INGREDIENTS	1 POUND	1.5 POUND	2 POUND
WHOLE WHEAT FLOUR	1 cup (120 g)	1 ½ cups (180 g)	2 cups (240 g)
BREAD FLOUR	¾ cup (90 g)	1 ⅛ cups (135 g)	1 ½ cups (180 g)
ROLLED OATS	¼ cup (30 g)	⅓ cup (40 g)	½ cup (60 g)
FLAXSEEDS	2 tbsps. (15 g)	3 tbsps. (22.5 g)	¼ cup (30 g)
SUNFLOWER SEEDS	2 tbsps. (15 g)	3 tbsps. (22.5 g)	¼ cup (30 g)
PUMPKIN SEEDS	2 tbsps. (15 g)	3 tbsps. (22.5 g)	¼ cup (30 g)
SESAME SEEDS	2 tbsps. (15 g)	3 tbsps. (22.5 g)	¼ cup (30 g)
ACTIVE DRY YEAST	½ packet (3.5 g)	¾ packet (5.25 g)	1 packet (7 g)
WARM WATER	¾ cup (180 ml)	1 cup (240 ml)	1 ¼ cups (300 ml)
HONEY	1 tbsp. (15 ml)	1 ½ tbsps. (22.5 ml)	2 tbsps. (30 ml)
OLIVE OIL	1 tbsp. (15 ml)	1 ½ tbsps. (22.5 ml)	2 tbsps. (30 ml)
SALT	½ tsp. (2.5 g)	¾ tsp. (3.75 g)	1 tsp. (5 g)

INSTRUCTIONS

1. In the bread machine pan, combine the whole wheat flour, bread flour, rolled oats, flaxseeds, sunflower seeds, pumpkin seeds, sesame seeds, and active dry yeast. Perform a thorough mixing to guarantee that the dry ingredients are distributed evenly.
2. Combine the warm water, honey, olive oil, and salt in another bowl until the honey is fully dissolved.
3. Pour the wet ingredients into the bread machine pan over the dry ingredients.
4. Place the bread machine pan into the bread machine and select the desired loaf size (one pound, one and a half, or two pounds) and additionally the whole wheat setting.
5. Start the bread machine and let it run through its cycle, including mixing, kneading, rising, and baking.
6. Once the baking cycle is complete, before slicing, carefully remove the bread from the bread machine pan and allow it to cool on a wire rack.

NUTRITION PER SERVING (1 SLICE): CALORIES 120; PROTEIN 5G; FAT 5G; CARBS 15G; FIBER 3G; SODIUM 120MG

MULTIGRAIN RYE BREAD

PREP TIME: 15 MINUTES
RISING TIME: 1-2 HOURS
BAKING TIME: APPROXIMATELY 1 HOUR
COMPLEXITY: BEGINNER

TOOL FUNCTION:
BREAD MAKER OPERATING SETTING:
WHOLE WHEAT SETTING
BAKING TEMPERATURE: 375°F (190°C)

TOOLS NEEDED:
BREAD MAKER
MEASURING CUPS AND SPOONS
MIXING BOWL

INGREDIENTS	1 POUND	1.5 POUND	2 POUND
RYE FLOUR	1 cup (120 g)	1 ½ cups (180 g)	2 cups (240 g)
BREAD FLOUR	1 cup (120 g)	1 ½ cups (180 g)	2 cups (240 g)
ROLLED OATS	¼ cup (30 g)	⅓ cup (40 g)	½ cup (60 g)
FLAXSEEDS	2 tbsps. (15 g)	3 tbsps. (22.5 g)	¼ cup (30 g)
SUNFLOWER SEEDS	2 tbsps. (15 g)	3 tbsps. (22.5 g)	¼ cup (30 g)
PUMPKIN SEEDS	2 tbsps. (15 g)	3 tbsps. (22.5 g)	¼ cup (30 g)
SESAME SEEDS	2 tbsps. (15 g)	3 tbsps. (22.5 g)	¼ cup (30 g)
ACTIVE DRY YEAST	½ packet (3.5 g)	¾ packet (5.25 g)	1 packet (7 g)
WARM WATER	¾ cup (180 ml)	1 cup (240 ml)	1 ¼ cups (300 ml)
HONEY	1 tbsp. (15 ml)	1 ½ tbsps. (22.5 ml)	2 tbsps. (30 ml)
OLIVE OIL	1 tbsp. (15 ml)	1 ½ tbsps. (22.5 ml)	2 tbsps. (30 ml)
SALT	½ tsp. (2.5 g)	¾ tsp. (3.75 g)	1 tsp. (5 g)

INSTRUCTIONS

1. Combine the rye flour, bread flour, rolled oats, flaxseeds, sunflower seeds, pumpkin seeds, sesame seeds, and active dry yeast in the bread machine pan. Perform a thorough mixing to guarantee that the dry ingredients are distributed evenly.
2. Combine the warm water, honey, olive oil, and salt in another bowl until the honey is fully dissolved.
3. Pour the wet ingredients into the bread machine pan over the dry ingredients.
4. Place the bread machine pan into the bread machine and select the desired loaf size (one pound, one and a half, or two pounds) and additionally the whole wheat setting.
5. Start the bread machine and let it run through its cycle, including mixing, kneading, rising, and baking.
6. Once the baking cycle is complete, before slicing, carefully remove the bread from the bread machine pan and allow it to cool on a wire rack.

NUTRITION PER SERVING (1 SLICE): CALORIES 110; PROTEIN 4G; FAT 4G; CARBS 15G; FIBER 3G; SODIUM 120M

SPICE, HERB, NUTS & VEGETABLE BREAD

ROSEMARY GARLIC BREAD

PREP TIME: 15 MINUTES
RISING TIME: 1-2 HOURS
BAKING TIME: APPROXIMATELY 1 HOUR
COMPLEXITY: BEGINNER

TOOL FUNCTION:
BREAD MAKER OPERATING SETTING:
BASIC/WHOLE WHEAT SETTING
BAKING TEMPERATURE: 375°F (190°C)

TOOLS NEEDED:
BREAD MAKER
MEASURING CUPS AND SPOONS
KNIFE AND CUTTING BOARD

INGREDIENTS	1 POUND	1.5 POUND	2 POUND
WARM WATER	¾ cup (180 ml)	1 ½ cups (360 ml)	2 cups (480 ml)
OLIVE OIL	1 ½ tbsps. (22 ml)	2 tbsps. (30 ml)	3 tbsps. (45 ml)
FRESH ROSEMARY	1 tbsp. (4 g)	1 ½ tbsps. (6 g)	2 tbsps. (8 g)
MINCED GARLIC	1 clove	1 clove	2 cloves
SALT	1 tsp. (5 g)	2 tsps. (10 g)	1 tbsp. (15 g)
BREAD FLOUR	2 cups (240 g)	3 cups (360 g)	4 cups (480 g)
SUGAR	1 tsp. (3 g)	1 tsp. (5 g)	2 tsps. (8 g)
ACTIVE DRY YEAST	1 tsp. (5 g)	2 tsps. (7 g)	2 ¼ tsps. (10 g)

INSTRUCTIONS

1. Fill the bread machine pan with all the ingredients in the order listed, starting with combining the liquids, followed by the dry ingredients, ensuring the yeast is added last, on top of the flour.
2. Select the Basic/Whole Wheat Setting on the bread maker and choose the desired loaf size (1 pound, 1.5 pounds, or 2 pounds).
3. Start the bread maker. The process of mixing the ingredients will begin.
4. Let the dough rise in the bread maker for approximately 1 hour or until it reaches the top of the pan.
5. Once the rising cycle is complete, the bread maker will automatically start the baking cycle.
6. After the baking cycle, before slicing, cool on a wire rack when it has been removed from the pan.

NUTRITION PER SERVING (1 SLICE):
CALORIES 120; PROTEIN 4G; FAT 3G; CARBS 20G; FIBER 3G; SODIUM 150MG

HONEY WALNUT BREAD

PREP TIME: 15 MINUTES
RISING TIME: 1-2 HOURS
BAKING TIME: APPROXIMATELY 1 HOUR
COMPLEXITY: BEGINNER

TOOL FUNCTION:
BREAD MAKER OPERATING SETTING:
BASIC/WHOLE WHEAT SETTING
BAKING TEMPERATURE: 375°F (190°C)

TOOLS NEEDED:
BREAD MAKER
MEASURING CUPS AND SPOONS
KNIFE AND CUTTING BOARD

INGREDIENTS	1 POUND	1.5 POUND	2 POUND
WARM WATER	½ cup (120 ml)	¾ cup (180 ml)	1 cup (240 ml)
OLIVE OIL	1 tbsp. (15 ml)	1 ½ tbsps. (22.5 ml)	2 tbsps. (30 ml)
HONEY	1 tbsp. (15 ml)	1 ½ tbsps. (22.5 ml)	2 tbsps. (30 ml)
SALT	½ tsp. (2.5 g)	¾ tsp. (3.75 g)	1 tsp. (5 g)
BREAD FLOUR	1 cup (120 g)	1 ½ cups (180 g)	2 cups (240 g)
WHOLE WHEAT FLOUR	½ cup (60 g)	¾ cup (90 g)	1 cup (120 g)
ACTIVE DRY YEAST	½ packet (3.5 g)	¾ packet (5.25 g)	1 packet (7 g)
CHOPPED WALNUTS	¼ cup (30 g)	⅓ cup (40 g)	½ cup (60 g)

INSTRUCTIONS

1. Fill the bread machine pan with all the ingredients in the order listed, starting with combining the liquids, followed by the dry ingredients, ensuring the yeast is added last, on top of the flour.
2. Select the Basic/Whole Wheat Setting on the bread maker and choose the desired loaf size (1 pound, 1.5 pounds, or 2 pounds).
3. Start the bread maker. The process of mixing the ingredients will begin.
4. Let the dough rise in the bread maker for approximately 1 hour or until it reaches the top of the pan.
5. Once the rising cycle is complete, the bread maker will automatically start the baking cycle.
6. Once the baking cycle is complete, before slicing, cool on a wire rack when it has been removed from the pan.

NUTRITION PER SERVING (1 SLICE): CALORIES 120; PROTEIN 4G; FAT 3G; CARBS 20G; FIBER 2G; SODIUM 150MG

SESAME GINGER BREAD

PREP TIME: 15 MINUTES
RISING TIME: 1-2 HOURS
BAKING TIME: APPROXIMATELY 1 HOUR
COMPLEXITY: BEGINNER

TOOL FUNCTION:
BREAD MAKER OPERATING SETTING:
BASIC/WHOLE WHEAT SETTING
BAKING TEMPERATURE: 375°F (190°C)

TOOLS NEEDED:
BREAD MAKER
MEASURING CUPS AND SPOONS
KNIFE AND CUTTING BOARD

INGREDIENTS	1 POUND	1.5 POUND	2 POUND
WARM WATER	½ cup (120 ml)	¾ cup (180 ml)	1 cup (240 ml)
OLIVE OIL	1 tbsp. (15 ml)	1 ½ tbsps. (22.5 ml)	2 tbsps. (30 ml)
HONEY	1 tbsp. (15 ml)	1 ½ tbsps. (22.5 ml)	2 tbsps. (30 ml)
SALT	½ tsp. (2.5 g)	¾ tsp. (3.75 g)	1 tsp. (5 g)
BREAD FLOUR	1 cup (120 g)	1 ½ cups (180 g)	2 cups (240 g)
WHOLE WHEAT FLOUR	½ cup (60 g)	¾ cup (90 g)	1 cup (120 g)
ACTIVE DRY YEAST	½ packet (3.5 g)	¾ packet (5.25 g)	1 packet (7 g)
TOASTED SESAME SEEDS	2 tbsps. (20 g)	3 tbsps. (30 g)	¼ cup (40 g)
MINCED GINGER	1 tbsp. (6 g)	1 ½ tbsps. (9 g)	2 tbsps. (12 g)

INSTRUCTIONS

1. Fill the bread machine pan with all the ingredients in the order listed, starting with combining the liquids, followed by the dry ingredients, ensuring the yeast is added last, on top of the flour.
2. Select the Basic/Whole Wheat Setting on the bread maker and choose the desired loaf size (1 pound, 1.5 pounds, or 2 pounds).
3. Start the bread maker. The process of mixing the ingredients will begin.
4. Let the dough rise in the bread maker for approximately 1 hour or until it reaches the top of the pan.
5. The bread maker will automatically start the baking cycle once the rising cycle is complete.
6. Once the baking cycle is complete, before slicing, cool on a wire rack when it has been removed from the pan.

NUTRITION PER SERVING (1 SLICE): CALORIES 110; PROTEIN 3G; FAT 3G; CARBS 18G; FIBER 2G; SODIUM 150MG

PESTO SWIRL BREAD

PREP TIME: 15 MINUTES
RISING TIME: 1-2 HOURS
BAKING TIME: APPROXIMATELY 1 HOUR
COMPLEXITY: BEGINNER

TOOL FUNCTION:
BREAD MAKER OPERATING SETTING:
BASIC/WHOLE WHEAT SETTING
BAKING TEMPERATURE: 375°F (190°C)

TOOLS NEEDED:
BREAD MAKER
MEASURING CUPS AND SPOONS
KNIFE AND CUTTING BOARD
ROLLING PIN
PASTRY BRUSH

INGREDIENTS	1 POUND	1.5 POUND	2 POUND
WATER	½ cup (120 ml)	¾ cup (180 ml)	1 cup (240 ml)
OLIVE OIL	1 tbsp. (15 ml)	1 ½ tbsps. (22.5 ml)	2 tbsps. (30 ml)
SALT	½ tsp. (2.5 g)	¾ tsp. (3.75 g)	1 tsp. (5 g)
SUGAR	1 tbsp. (15 g)	1 ½ tbsps. (22.5 g)	2 tbsps. (30 g)
BREAD FLOUR	1 cup (120 g)	1 ½ cups (180 g)	2 cups (240 g)
WHOLE WHEAT FLOUR	½ cup (60 g)	¾ cup (90 g)	1 cup (120 g)
ACTIVE DRY YEAST	½ packet (3.5 g)	¾ packet (5.25 g)	1 packet (7 g)
PESTO SAUCE	2 tbsps. (30 g)	3 tbsps. (45 g)	¼ cup (60 g)

INSTRUCTIONS

1. In a bread pan, combine water, olive oil, salt, sugar, bread flour, whole wheat flour, and active dry yeast.
2. Select your desired loaf size (1 lb, 1.5 lb, or 2 lb) and the Basic/Whole Wheat bread machine setting.
3. Start the bread maker and let it cycle through stirring, kneading, and rising.
4. Remove and roll the dough on a lightly floured surface into a rectangle after kneading.
5. Spread the pesto evenly over the rolled-out dough.
6. Roll the dough tightly at one end to form a log.
7. With a well-edged blade, slice the log into pieces.
8. Carefully place the dough slices into the loaf pan in a single layer.
9. Close the lid and allow the bread maker to continue the baking cycle.
10. Once the baking cycle is complete, carefully remove the bread from the bread maker, then let it cool on a cooling rack before slicing and serving.

NUTRITION PER SERVING (1 SLICE): CALORIES 110; PROTEIN 2G; FAT 3G; CARBS 16G; FIBER 2G; SODIUM 200MG

MAPLE WALNUT BREAD

PREP TIME: 15 MINUTES
RISING TIME: 1-2 HOURS
BAKING TIME: APPROXIMATELY 1 HOUR
COMPLEXITY: BEGINNER

TOOL FUNCTION:
BREAD MAKER OPERATING SETTING:
BASIC/WHOLE WHEAT SETTING
BAKING TEMPERATURE: 375°F (190°C)

TOOLS NEEDED:
BREAD MAKER
MEASURING CUPS AND SPOONS
KNIFE AND CUTTING BOARD

INGREDIENTS	1 POUND	1.5 POUND	2 POUND
WARM WATER	½ cup (120 ml)	¾ cup (180 ml)	1 cup (240 ml)
OLIVE OIL	1 tbsp. (15 ml)	1 ½ tbsps. (22.5 ml)	2 tbsps. (30 ml)
SALT	½ tsp. (2.5 g)	¾ tsp. (3.75 g)	1 tsp. (5 g)
SUGAR	1 tbsp. (15 g)	1 ½ tbsps. (22.5 g)	2 tbsps. (30 g)
BREAD FLOUR	1 cup (120 g)	1 ½ cups (180 g)	2 cups (240 g)
WHOLE WHEAT FLOUR	½ cup (60 g)	¾ cup (90 g)	1 cup (120 g)
ACTIVE DRY YEAST	½ packet (3.5 g)	¾ packet (5.25 g)	1 packet (7 g)
CHOPPED MAPLE-GLAZED WALNUTS	¼ cup (30 g)	⅓ cup (40 g)	½ cup (60 g)

INSTRUCTIONS

1. Fill the bread machine pan with all the ingredients in the order listed, starting with combining the liquids, followed by the dry ingredients, ensuring the yeast is added last, on top of the flour.
2. Select the Basic/Whole Wheat Setting on the bread maker and choose the desired loaf size (1 pound, 1.5 pounds, or 2 pounds).
3. Start the bread maker. The process of mixing the ingredients will begin.
4. Let the dough rise in the bread maker for approximately 1 hour or until it reaches the top of the pan.
5. The bread maker will automatically start the baking cycle once the rising cycle is complete.
6. Once the baking cycle is complete, before slicing, cool on a wire rack when it has been removed from the pan.

NUTRITION PER SERVING (1 SLICE): CALORIES 120; PROTEIN 4G; FAT 3G; CARBS 20G; FIBER 2G; SODIUM 150MG

LAVENDER HONEY BREAD

PREP TIME: 15 MINUTES
RISING TIME: 1-2 HOURS
BAKING TIME: APPROXIMATELY 1 HOUR
COMPLEXITY: BEGINNER

TOOL FUNCTION:
BREAD MAKER OPERATING SETTING:
BASIC/WHOLE WHEAT SETTING
BAKING TEMPERATURE: 375°F (190°C)

TOOLS NEEDED:
BREAD MAKER
MEASURING CUPS AND SPOONS

INGREDIENTS	1 POUND	1.5 POUND	2 POUND
WARM WATER	½ cup (120 ml)	¾ cup (180 ml)	1 cup (240 ml)
OLIVE OIL	1 tbsp. (15 ml)	1 ½ tbsps. (22.5 ml)	2 tbsps. (30 ml)
SALT	½ tsp. (2.5 g)	¾ tsp. (3.75 g)	1 tsp. (5 g)
HONEY	1 tbsp. (15 g)	1 ½ tbsps. (22.5 g)	2 tbsps. (30 g)
BREAD FLOUR	1 cup (120 g)	1 ½ cups (180 g)	2 cups (240 g)
WHOLE WHEAT FLOUR	½ cup (60 g)	¾ cup (90 g)	1 cup (120 g)
ACTIVE DRY YEAST	½ packet (3.5 g)	¾ packet (5.25 g)	1 packet (7 g)
DRIED LAVENDER FLOWERS	1 tbsp. (2 g)	1 ½ tbsps. (3 g)	2 tbsps. (4 g)

INSTRUCTIONS

1. Fill the bread machine pan with all the ingredients in the order listed, starting with combining the liquids, followed by the dry ingredients, ensuring the yeast is added last, on top of the flour.
2. Select the Basic/Whole Wheat Setting on the bread maker and choose the desired loaf size (1 pound, 1.5 pounds, or 2 pounds).
3. Start the bread maker. The process of mixing the ingredients will begin.
4. Let the dough rise in the bread maker for approximately 1 hour or until it reaches the top of the pan.
5. The bread maker will automatically start the baking cycle once the rising cycle is complete.
6. After the baking cycle, before slicing, cool on a wire rack when it has been removed from the pan.

- -

NUTRITION PER SERVING (1 SLICE): CALORIES 110; PROTEIN 3G; FAT 2G; CARBS 20G; FIBER 2G; SODIUM 140MG

GINGERBREAD LOAF

PREP TIME: 15 MINUTES
RISING TIME: 1-2 HOURS
BAKING TIME: APPROXIMATELY 1 HOUR
COMPLEXITY: BEGINNER

TOOL FUNCTION:
BREAD MAKER OPERATING SETTING:
BASIC/WHOLE WHEAT SETTING
BAKING TEMPERATURE: 375°F (190°C)

TOOLS NEEDED:
BREAD MAKER
MEASURING CUPS AND SPOONS
KNIFE AND CUTTING BOARD

INGREDIENTS	1 POUND	1.5 POUND	2 POUND
WARM WATER	½ cup (120 ml)	¾ cup (180 ml)	1 cup (240 ml)
VEGETABLE OIL	1 tbsp. (15 ml)	1 ½ tbsps. (22.5 ml)	2 tbsps. (30 ml)
SALT	½ tsp. (2.5 g)	¾ tsp. (3.75 g)	1 tsp. (5 g)
MOLASSES	1 tbsp. (20 g)	1 ½ tbsps. (30 g)	2 tbsps. (40 g)
GROUND GINGER	1 tsp. (5 g)	1 ½ tsps. (7.5 g)	2 tsps. (10 g)
GROUND CINNAMON	1 tsp. (2 g)	1 ½ tsps. (3 g)	2 tsps. (4 g)
GROUND CLOVES	¼ tsp. (0.5 g)	⅜ tsp. (0.75 g)	½ tsp. (1 g)
BREAD FLOUR	1 cup (120 g)	1 ½ cups (180 g)	2 cups (240 g)
WHOLE WHEAT FLOUR	½ cup (60 g)	¾ cup (90 g)	1 cup (120 g)
ACTIVE DRY YEAST	½ packet (3.5 g)	¾ packet (5.25 g)	1 packet (7 g)

INSTRUCTIONS

1. Fill the bread machine pan with all the ingredients in the order listed, starting with combining the liquids, followed by the dry ingredients, ensuring the yeast is added last, on top of the flour.
2. Select the Basic/Whole Wheat Setting on the bread maker and choose the desired loaf size (1 pound, 1.5 pounds, or 2 pounds).
3. Start the bread maker. The process of mixing the ingredients will begin.
4. Let the dough rise in the bread maker for approximately 1 hour or until it reaches the top of the pan.
5. The bread maker will automatically start the baking cycle once the rising cycle is complete.
6. After the baking cycle, before slicing, cool on a wire rack when it has been removed from the pan.

- -

NUTRITION PER SERVING (1 SLICE): CALORIES 110; PROTEIN 3G; FAT 2G; CARBS 20G; FIBER 2G; SODIUM 140MG

FENNEL RYE BREAD

PREP TIME: 15 MINUTES
RISING TIME: 1-2 HOURS
BAKING TIME: APPROXIMATELY 1 HOUR
COMPLEXITY: BEGINNER

TOOL FUNCTION:
BREAD MAKER OPERATING SETTING:
BASIC/WHOLE WHEAT SETTING
BAKING TEMPERATURE: 375°F (190°C)

TOOLS NEEDED:
BREAD MAKER
MEASURING CUPS AND SPOONS

INGREDIENTS	1 POUND	1.5 POUND	2 POUND
WARM WATER	½ cup (120 ml)	¾ cup (180 ml)	1 cup (240 ml)
OLIVE OIL	1 tbsp. (15 ml)	1 ½ tbsps. (22.5 ml)	2 tbsps. (30 ml)
SALT	½ tsp. (2.5 g)	¾ tsp. (3.75 g)	1 tsp. (5 g)
SUGAR	1 tbsp. (15 g)	1 ½ tbsps. (22.5 g)	2 tbsps. (30 g)
DARK RYE FLOUR	1 cup (120 g)	1 ½ cups (180 g)	2 cups (240 g)
BREAD FLOUR	½ cup (60 g)	¾ cup (90 g)	1 cup (120 g)
ACTIVE DRY YEAST	½ packet (3.5 g)	¾ packet (5.25 g)	1 packet (7 g)
TOASTED FENNEL SEEDS	2 tbsps. (10 g)	3 tbsps. (15 g)	¼ cup (40 g)

INSTRUCTIONS

1. Fill the bread machine pan with all the ingredients in the order listed, starting with combining the liquids, followed by the dry ingredients, ensuring the yeast is added last, on top of the flour.
2. Select the Basic/Whole Wheat Setting on the bread maker and choose the desired loaf size (1 pound, 1.5 pounds, or 2 pounds).
3. Start the bread maker. The process of mixing the ingredients will begin.
4. Let the dough rise in the bread maker for approximately 1 hour or until it reaches the top of the pan.
5. The bread maker will automatically start the baking cycle once the rising cycle is complete.
6. After the baking cycle, before slicing, cool on a wire rack when it has been removed from the pan.

NUTRITION PER SERVING (1 SLICE): CALORIES 110; PROTEIN 3G; FAT 2G; CARBS 20G; FIBER 2G; SODIUM 140MG

COCONUT CURRY BREAD

PREP TIME: 15 MINUTES
RISING TIME: 1-2 HOURS
BAKING TIME: APPROXIMATELY 1 HOUR
COMPLEXITY: BEGINNER

TOOL FUNCTION:
BREAD MAKER OPERATING SETTING:
BASIC/WHOLE WHEAT SETTING
BAKING TEMPERATURE: 375°F (190°C)

TOOLS NEEDED:
BREAD MAKER
MEASURING CUPS AND SPOONS

INGREDIENTS	1 POUND	1.5 POUND	2 POUND
WARM WATER	½ cup (120 ml)	¾ cup (180 ml)	1 cup (240 ml)
COCONUT OIL	2 tbsps. (30 ml)	3 tbsps. (45 ml)	¼ cup (60 ml)
SALT	1 tsp. (5 g)	1 ½ tsps. (7.5 g)	2 tsps. (10 g)
SHREDDED COCONUT	2 tbsps. (15 g)	3 tbsps. (22.5 g)	¼ cup (30 g)
CURRY POWDER	1 tsp. (2 g)	1 ½ tsps. (3 g)	2 tsps. (4 g)
BREAD FLOUR	1 ½ cups (180 g)	2 ¼ cups (270 g)	3 cups (360 g)
WHOLE WHEAT FLOUR	½ cup (60 g)	¾ cup (90 g)	1 cup (120 g)
ACTIVE DRY YEAST	1 packet (7 g)	1 ½ packets (10.5 g)	2 packets (14 g)

INSTRUCTIONS

1. Fill the bread machine pan with all the ingredients in the order listed, starting with combining the liquids, followed by the dry ingredients, ensuring the yeast is added last, on top of the flour.
2. Select the Basic/Whole Wheat Setting on the bread maker and choose the desired loaf size (1 pound, 1.5 pounds, or 2 pounds).
3. Start the bread maker. The process of mixing the ingredients will begin.
4. Let the dough rise in the bread maker for approximately 1 hour or until it reaches the top of the pan.
5. Once the rising cycle is complete, the bread maker will automatically start the baking cycle.
6. After the baking cycle, before slicing, cool on a wire rack when it has been removed from the pan.

NUTRITION PER SERVING (1 SLICE): CALORIES 140; PROTEIN 3G; FAT 7G; CARBS 20G; FIBER 2G; SODIUM 140MG

SAFFRON RAISIN BREAD

PREP TIME: 15 MINUTES
RISING TIME: 1-2 HOURS
BAKING TIME: APPROXIMATELY 1 HOUR
COMPLEXITY: BEGINNER

TOOL FUNCTION:
BREAD MAKER OPERATING SETTING:
BASIC/WHOLE WHEAT SETTING
BAKING TEMPERATURE: 375°F (190°C)

TOOLS NEEDED:
BREAD MAKER
MEASURING CUPS AND SPOONS

INGREDIENTS	1 POUND	1.5 POUND	2 POUND
WARM WATER	½ cup (120 ml)	¾ cup (180 ml)	1 cup (240 ml)
OLIVE OIL	2 tbsps. (30 ml)	3 tbsps. (45 ml)	¼ cup (60 ml)
SALT	1 tsp. (5 g)	1 ½ tsps. (7.5 g)	2 tsps. (10 g)
SAFFRON THREADS	1 pinch	2 pinches	3 pinches
RAISINS	¼ cup (40 g)	⅓ cup (55 g)	½ cup (80 g)
BREAD FLOUR	1 ½ cups (180 g)	2 ¼ cups (270 g)	3 cups (360 g)
WHOLE WHEAT FLOUR	½ cup (60 g)	¾ cup (90 g)	1 cup (120 g)
ACTIVE DRY YEAST	1 packet (7 g)	1 ½ packets (10.5 g)	2 packets (14 g)

INSTRUCTIONS

1. Fill the bread machine pan with all the ingredients in the order listed, starting with combining the liquids, followed by the dry ingredients, ensuring the yeast is added last, on top of the flour.
2. Select the Basic/Whole Wheat Setting on the bread maker and choose the desired loaf size (1 pound, 1.5 pounds, or 2 pounds).
3. Start the bread maker. The process of mixing the ingredients will begin.
4. Let the dough rise in the bread maker for approximately 1 hour or until it reaches the top of the pan.
5. The bread maker will automatically start the baking cycle once the rising cycle is complete.
6. After the baking cycle, before slicing, cool on a wire rack when it has been removed from the pan.

- -

NUTRITION PER SERVING (1 SLICE): CALORIES 110; PROTEIN 3G; FAT 2G; CARBS 20G; FIBER 2G; SODIUM 140MG

CHILI LIME CORNBREAD

PREP TIME: 15 MINUTES
RISING TIME: 1-2 HOURS
BAKING TIME: APPROXIMATELY 1 HOUR
COMPLEXITY: BEGINNER

TOOL FUNCTION:
BREAD MAKER OPERATING SETTING:
BASIC/WHOLE WHEAT SETTING
BAKING TEMPERATURE: 375°F (190°C)

TOOLS NEEDED:
BREAD MAKER
MEASURING CUPS AND SPOONS
KNIFE AND CUTTING BOARD

INGREDIENTS	1 POUND	1.5 POUND	2 POUND
WARM WATER	¾ cup (180 ml)	1 ⅛ cups (270 ml)	1 ½ cups (360 ml)
VEGETABLE OIL	2 tbsps. (30 ml)	3 tbsps. (45 ml)	¼ cup (60 ml)
SALT	1 tsp. (5 g)	1 ½ tsps. (7.5 g)	2 tsps. (10 g)
LIME ZEST	Zest of 1 lime	Zest of 2 limes	Zest of 3 limes
GREEN CHILIES	¼ cup (30 g)	⅓ cup (50 g)	½ cup (80 g)
CORN KERNELS	¼ cup (40 g)	⅓ cup (55 g)	½ cup (80 g)
CORNMEAL	1 ½ cups (180 g)	2 ¼ cups (270 g)	3 cups (360 g)
ALL-PURPOSE FLOUR	½ cup (60 g)	¾ cup (90 g)	1 cup (120 g)
ACTIVE DRY YEAST	1 packet (7 g)	1 ½ packets (10.5 g)	2 packets (14 g)

INSTRUCTIONS

1. Fill the bread maker pan with all the ingredients in the order listed, starting with combining the liquids, followed by the dry ingredients, ensuring the yeast is added last, on top of the flour.
2. Select the Basic/Whole Wheat Setting on the bread maker and choose the desired loaf size (1 pound, 1.5 pounds, or 2 pounds).
3. Start the bread maker. The process of mixing the ingredients will begin.
4. Let the dough rise in the bread maker for approximately 1 hour or until it reaches the top of the pan.
5. Once the rising cycle is complete, the bread maker will automatically start the baking cycle.
6. Once the baking cycle is complete, before slicing, cool on a wire rack when it has been removed from the pan.

NUTRITION PER SERVING (1 SLICE): CALORIES 110; PROTEIN 3G; FAT 2G; CARBS 20G; FIBER 2G; SODIUM 140MG

MUSHROOM THYME BREAD

PREP TIME: 15 MINUTES
RISING TIME: 1-2 HOURS
BAKING TIME: APPROXIMATELY 1 HOUR
COMPLEXITY: BEGINNER

TOOL FUNCTION:
BREAD MAKER OPERATING SETTING:
BASIC/WHOLE WHEAT SETTING
BAKING TEMPERATURE: 375°F (190°C)

TOOLS NEEDED:
BREAD MAKER
MEASURING CUPS AND SPOONS
KNIFE AND CUTTING BOARD

INGREDIENTS	1 POUND	1.5 POUND	2 POUND
WARM WATER	¾ cup (180 ml)	1 ⅛ cups (270 ml)	1 ½ cups (360 ml)
OLIVE OIL	2 tbsps. (30 ml)	3 tbsps. (45 ml)	¼ cup (60 ml)
SALT	1 tsp. (5 g)	1 ½ tsps. (7.5 g)	2 tsps. (10 g)
BREAD FLOUR	1 cup (120 g)	1 ½ cups (180 g)	2 cups (240 g)
WHOLE WHEAT FLOUR	½ cup (60 g)	¾ cup (90 g)	1 cup (120 g)
ACTIVE DRY YEAST	½ packet (3.5 g)	¾ packet (5.25 g)	1 packet (7 g)
SAUTÉED MUSHROOMS	½ cup (60 g)	¾ cup (90 g)	1 cup (120 g)
FRESH THYME LEAVES	1 tbsp. (2 g)	1 ½ tbsps. (3 g)	2 tbsps. (4 g)

INSTRUCTIONS

1. Fill the bread machine pan with all the ingredients in the order listed, starting with combining the liquids, followed by the dry ingredients, ensuring the yeast is added last, on top of the flour.
2. Select the Basic/Whole Wheat Setting on the bread maker and choose the desired loaf size (1 pound, 1.5 pounds, or 2 pounds).
3. Start the bread maker. The process of mixing the ingredients will begin.
4. Let the dough rise in the bread maker for approximately 1 hour or until it reaches the top of the pan.
5. Once the rising cycle is complete, the bread maker will automatically start the baking cycle.
6. Once the baking cycle is complete, before slicing, cool on a wire rack when it has been removed from the pan.

NUTRITION PER SERVING (1 SLICE): CALORIES 110; PROTEIN 3G; FAT 2G; CARBS 20G; FIBER 2G; SODIUM 140MG

CHEESE BREAD

CLASSIC CHEDDAR CHEESE BREAD

PREP TIME: 15 MINUTES
RISING TIME: 1-2 HOURS
BAKING TIME: APPROXIMATELY 1 HOUR
COMPLEXITY: BEGINNER

TOOL FUNCTION:
BREAD MAKER OPERATING SETTING:
BASIC/WHOLE WHEAT SETTING
BAKING TEMPERATURE: 375°F (190°C)

TOOLS NEEDED:
BREAD MAKER
MEASURING CUPS AND SPOONS

INGREDIENTS	1 POUND	1.5 POUND	2 POUND
WARM MILK	½ cup (120 ml)	¾ cup (180 ml)	1 cup (240 ml)
UNSALTED BUTTER	1 tbsp. (15 g)	1 ½ tbsps. (22.5 g)	2 tbsps. (30 g)
BREAD FLOUR	1 ½ cups (180 g)	2 ¼ cups (270 g)	3 cups (360 g)
SALT	¾ tsp. (3.5 g)	1 ⅛ tsps. (5.25 g)	1 ½ tsps. (7 g)
GRANULATED SUGAR	1 tbsp. (15 g)	1 ½ tbsps. (22.5 g)	2 tbsps. (30 g)
ACTIVE DRY YEAST	¾ tsp. (3.5 g)	1 ⅛ tsps. (5.25 g)	1 ½ tsps. (7 g)
SHREDDED CHEDDAR CHEESE	¾ cup (90 g)	1 ⅛ cups (135 g)	1 ½ cups (180 g)

INSTRUCTIONS

1. Fill the bread machine pan with all the ingredients in the order listed, starting with combining the liquids, followed by the dry ingredients, ensuring the yeast is added last, on top of the flour.
2. Select the Basic/Whole Wheat Setting on the bread maker and choose the desired loaf size (1 pound, 1.5 pounds, or 2 pounds).
3. Start the bread maker. The process of mixing the ingredients will begin.
4. Let the dough rise in the bread maker for approximately 1 hour or until it reaches the top of the pan.
5. The bread maker will automatically start the baking cycle once the rising cycle is complete.
6. After the baking cycle, before slicing, cool on a wire rack when it has been removed from the pan.

NUTRITION PER SERVING (1 SLICE): CALORIES 110; FAT 4G; CARBS 15G; PROTEIN 5G; FIBER 1G; SODIUM 200MG

ASIAGO AND SUN-DRIED TOMATO BREAD

PREP TIME: 10 MINUTES
RISING TIME: 1-2 HOURS
BAKING TIME: APPROXIMATELY 1 HOUR
COMPLEXITY: BEGINNER

TOOL FUNCTION:
BREAD MAKER OPERATING SETTING:
BASIC/WHOLE WHEAT SETTING
BAKING TEMPERATURE: 375°F (190°C)

TOOLS NEEDED:
BREAD MAKER
MEASURING CUPS AND
SPOONS

INGREDIENTS	1 POUND	1.5 POUND	2 POUND
WARM MILK	½ cup (120 ml)	¾ cup (180 ml)	1 cup (240 ml)
UNSALTED BUTTER, SOFTENED	1 tbsp. (15 g)	1 ½ tbsps. (22.5 g)	2 tbsps. (30 g)
BREAD FLOUR	1 ½ cups (180 g)	2 ¼ cups (270 g)	3 cups (360 g)
GRANULATED SUGAR	½ tbsp. (7.5 g)	1 tbsp. (15 g)	1 tbsp. (15 g)
SALT	¾ tsp. (3.5 g)	1 ⅛ tsps. (5.25 g)	1 ½ tsps. (7 g)
CHOPPED SUN-DRIED TOMATOES	¼ cup (30 g)	⅓ cup (40 g)	½ cup (60 g)
ACTIVE DRY YEAST	¾ tsp. (3.5 g)	1 ⅛ tsps. (5.25 g)	1 ½ tsps. (7 g)
GRATED ASIAGO CHEESE	½ cup (60 g)	¾ cup (90 g)	1 cup (120 g)

INSTRUCTIONS

1. Fill the bread maker pan with all the ingredients in the order listed, starting with combining the liquids, followed by the dry ingredients, ensuring the yeast is added last, on top of the flour.
2. Select the Basic/Whole Wheat Setting on the bread maker and choose the desired loaf size (1 pound, 1.5 pounds, or 2 pounds).
3. Start the bread maker. The process of mixing the ingredients will begin.
4. Let the dough rise in the bread maker for approximately 1 hour or until it reaches the top of the pan.
5. The bread maker will automatically start the baking cycle once the rising cycle is complete.
6. After the baking cycle, before slicing, cool on a wire rack when it has been removed from the pan.

NUTRITION PER SERVING (1 SLICE): CALORIES 110; FAT 4G; CARBS 15G; PROTEIN 5G; FIBER 1G; SODIUM 200MG

GOUDA AND CARAMELIZED ONION BREAD

PREP TIME: 10 MINUTES
RISING TIME: 1-2 HOURS
BAKING TIME: APPROXIMATELY 1 HOUR
COMPLEXITY: BEGINNER

TOOL FUNCTION:
BREAD MAKER OPERATING SETTING:
BASIC/WHOLE WHEAT SETTING
BAKING TEMPERATURE: 375°F (190°C)

TOOLS NEEDED:
BREAD MAKER
MEASURING CUPS AND
SPOONS

INGREDIENTS	1 POUND	1.5 POUND	2 POUND
WARM WATER	½ cup (120 ml)	¾ cup (180 ml)	1 cup (240 ml)
OLIVE OIL	1 tbsp. (15 g)	1 ½ tbsps. (22.5 g)	2 tbsps. (30 g)
BREAD FLOUR	1 ½ cups (180 g)	2 ¼ cups (270 g)	3 cups (360 g)
GRANULATED SUGAR	½ tbsp. (7.5 g)	1 tbsp. (15 g)	1 tbsp. (15 g)
SALT	¾ tsp. (3.5 g)	1 ⅛ tsps. (5.25 g)	1 ½ tsps. (7 g)
SHREDDED GOUDA CHEESE	½ cup (75 g)	¾ cup (110 g)	1 cup (150 g)
CARAMELIZED ONIONS	½ cup (75 g)	¾ cup (110 g)	1 cup (150 g)
ACTIVE DRY YEAST	¾ tsp. (3.5 g)	1 ⅛ tsps. (5.25 g)	1 ½ tsps. (7 g)

INSTRUCTIONS

1. Fill the bread maker pan with all the ingredients in the order listed, starting with combining the liquids, followed by the dry ingredients, ensuring the yeast is added last, on top of the flour.
2. Select the Basic/Whole Wheat Setting on the bread maker and choose the desired loaf size (1 pound, 1.5 pounds, or 2 pounds).
3. Start the bread maker. The process of mixing the ingredients will begin.
4. Let the dough rise in the bread maker for approximately 1 hour or until it reaches the top of the pan.
5. The bread maker will automatically start the baking cycle once the rising cycle is complete.
6. After the baking cycle, before slicing, cool on a wire rack when it has been removed from the pan.

NUTRITION PER SERVING (1 SLICE): CALORIES 110; FAT 4G; CARBS 18G; PROTEIN 4G; FIBER 1G; SODIUM 200MG

BLUE CHEESE AND WALNUT BREAD

PREP TIME: 10 MINUTES
RISING TIME: 1-2 HOURS
BAKING TIME: APPROXIMATELY 1 HOUR
COMPLEXITY: BEGINNER

TOOL FUNCTION:
BREAD MAKER OPERATING SETTING:
BASIC/WHOLE WHEAT SETTING
BAKING TEMPERATURE: 375°F (190°C)

TOOLS NEEDED:
BREAD MAKER
MEASURING CUPS AND
SPOONS
KNIFE AND CUTTING BOARD

INGREDIENTS	1 POUND	1.5 POUND	2 POUND
WARM MILK	½ cup (120 ml)	¾ cup (180 ml)	1 cup (240 ml)
UNSALTED BUTTER, SOFTENED	1 tbsp. (15 g)	1 ½ tbsps. (22.5 g)	2 tbsps. (30 g)
BREAD FLOUR	1 ½ cups (180 g)	2 ¼ cups (270 g)	3 cups (360 g)
GRANULATED SUGAR	½ tbsp. (7.5 g)	1 tbsp. (15 g)	1 tbsp. (15 g)
SALT	¾ tsp. (3.5 g)	1 ⅛ tsps. (5.25 g)	1 ½ tsps. (7 g)
CRUMBLED BLUE CHEESE	½ cup (60 g)	¾ cup (90 g)	1 cup (120 g)
CHOPPED WALNUTS	¼ cup (30 g)	⅓ cup (40 g)	½ cup (60 g)
ACTIVE DRY YEAST	¾ tsp. (3.5 g)	1 ⅛ tsps. (5.25 g)	1 ½ tsps. (7 g)

INSTRUCTIONS

1. Fill the bread maker pan with all the ingredients in the order listed, starting with combining the liquids, followed by the dry ingredients, ensuring the yeast is added last, on top of the flour.
2. Select the Basic/Whole Wheat Setting on the bread maker and choose the desired loaf size (1 pound, 1.5 pounds, or 2 pounds).
3. Start the bread maker. The process of mixing the ingredients will begin.
4. Let the dough rise in the bread maker for approximately 1 hour or until it reaches the top of the pan.
5. The bread maker will automatically start the baking cycle once the rising cycle is complete.
6. After the baking cycle, before slicing, cool on a wire rack when it has been removed from the pan.

- -

NUTRITION PER SERVING (1 SLICE): CALORIES 110; FAT 4G; CARBS 15G; PROTEIN 4G; FIBER 1G; SODIUM 220M

SWISS CHEESE AND HAM BREAD

PREP TIME: 10 MINUTES
RISING TIME: 1-2 HOURS
BAKING TIME: APPROXIMATELY 1 HOUR
COMPLEXITY: BEGINNER

TOOL FUNCTION:
BREAD MAKER OPERATING
SETTING: BASIC/WHOLE WHEAT
SETTING
BAKING TEMPERATURE: 375°F
(190°C)

TOOLS NEEDED:
BREAD MAKER
MEASURING CUPS AND SPOONS
KNIFE AND CUTTING BOARD

INGREDIENTS	1 POUND	1.5 POUND	2 POUND
WARM WATER	½ cup (120 ml)	¾ cup (180 ml)	1 cup (240 ml)
OLIVE OIL	1 tbsp. (15 g)	1 ½ tbsps. (22.5 g)	2 tbsps. (30 g)
BREAD FLOUR	1 ½ cups (180 g)	2 ¼ cups (270 g)	3 cups (360 g)
GRANULATED SUGAR	½ tbsp. (7.5 g)	1 tbsp. (15 g)	1 tbsp. (15 g)
SALT	¾ tsp. (3.5 g)	1 ⅛ tsps. (5.25 g)	1 ½ tsps. (7 g)
SHREDDED SWISS CHEESE	½ cup (75 g)	¾ cup (112.5 g)	1 cup (150 g)
DICED HAM	¼ cup (37.5 g)	⅓ cup (50 g)	½ cup (75 g)
ACTIVE DRY YEAST	¾ tsp. (3.5 g)	1 ⅛ tsps. (5.25 g)	1 ½ tsps. (7 g)

INSTRUCTIONS

1. Fill the bread maker pan with all the ingredients in the order listed, starting with adding the liquids, followed by the dry components, ensuring the yeast is added last, on top of the flour.
2. Select the Basic/Whole Wheat Setting on the bread maker and choose the desired loaf size (1 pound, 1.5 pounds, or 2 pounds).
3. Start the bread maker. The process of mixing the ingredients will begin.
4. Let the dough rise in the bread maker for approximately 1 hour or until it reaches the top of the pan.
5. The bread maker will automatically start the baking cycle once the rising cycle is complete.
6. After the baking cycle, before slicing, cool on a wire rack when it has been removed from the pan.

NUTRITION PER SERVING (1 SLICE): CALORIES 120; FAT 3G; CARBS 18G; PROTEIN 6G; FIBER 1G; SODIUM 300MG

FETA AND OLIVE BREAD

PREP TIME: 10 MINUTES
RISING TIME: 1-2 HOURS
BAKING TIME: APPROXIMATELY 1 HOUR
COMPLEXITY: BEGINNER

TOOL FUNCTION:
BREAD MAKER OPERATING SETTING:
BASIC/WHOLE WHEAT SETTING
BAKING TEMPERATURE: 375°F (190°C)

TOOLS NEEDED:
BREAD MAKER
MEASURING CUPS AND
SPOONS
KNIFE AND CUTTING BOARD

INGREDIENTS	1 POUND	1.5 POUND	2 POUND
WARM MILK	½ cup (120 ml)	¾ cup (180 ml)	1 cup (240 ml)
UNSALTED BUTTER	1 tbsp. (15 g)	1 ½ tbsps. (22.5 g)	2 tbsps. (30 g)
BREAD FLOUR	1 ½ cups (180 g)	2 ¼ cups (270 g)	3 cups (360 g)
GRANULATED SUGAR	½ tbsp. (7.5 g)	1 tbsp. (15 g)	1 tbsp. (15 g)
SALT	¾ tsp. (3.5 g)	1 ⅛ tsps. (5.25 g)	1 ½ tsps. (7 g)
CRUMBLED FETA CHEESE	½ cup (75 g)	¾ cup (112.5 g)	1 cup (150 g)
CHOPPED OLIVES	¼ cup (37.5 g)	⅓ cup (50 g)	½ cup (75 g)
ACTIVE DRY YEAST	¾ tsp. (3.5 g)	1 ⅛ tsps. (5.25 g)	1 ½ tsps. (7 g)

INSTRUCTIONS

1. Fill the bread maker pan with all the ingredients in the order listed, starting with adding the liquids, followed by the dry components, ensuring the yeast is added last, on top of the flour.
2. Select the Basic/Whole Wheat Setting on the bread maker and choose the desired loaf size (1 pound, 1.5 pounds, or 2 pounds).
3. Start the bread maker. The process of mixing the ingredients will begin.
4. Let the dough rise in the bread maker for approximately 1 hour or until it reaches the top of the pan.
5. The bread maker will automatically start the baking cycle once the rising cycle is complete.
6. After the baking cycle, before slicing, cool on a wire rack when it has been removed from the pan.

NUTRITION PER SERVING (1 SLICE): CALORIES 120; FAT 3G; CARBS 18G; PROTEIN 6G; FIBER 1G; SODIUM 300MG

MOZZARELLA AND BASIL BREAD

PREP TIME: 10 MINUTES
RISING TIME: 1-2 HOURS
BAKING TIME: APPROXIMATELY 1 HOUR
COMPLEXITY: BEGINNER

TOOL FUNCTION:
BREAD MAKER OPERATING SETTING:
BASIC/WHOLE WHEAT SETTING
BAKING TEMPERATURE: 375°F (190°C)

TOOLS NEEDED:
BREAD MAKER
MEASURING CUPS AND SPOONS
KNIFE AND CUTTING BOARD

INGREDIENTS	1 POUND	1.5 POUND	2 POUND
WARM WATER	½ cup (120 ml)	¾ cup (180 ml)	1 cup (240 ml)
OLIVE OIL	1 tbsp. (15 g)	1 ½ tbsps. (22.5 g)	2 tbsps. (30 g)
BREAD FLOUR	1 ½ cups (180 g)	2 ¼ cups (270 g)	3 cups (360 g)
GRANULATED SUGAR	½ tbsp. (7.5 g)	1 tbsp. (15 g)	1 tbsp. (15 g)
SALT	¾ tsp. (3.5 g)	1 ⅛ tsps. (5.25 g)	1 ½ tsps. (7 g)
SHREDDED MOZZARELLA CHEESE	½ cup (75 g)	¾ cup (112.5 g)	1 cup (150 g)
CHOPPED FRESH BASIL	¼ cup (15 g)	⅓ cup (20 g)	½ cup (30 g)
ACTIVE DRY YEAST	¾ tsp. (3.5 g)	1 ⅛ tsps. (5.25 g)	1 ½ tsps. (7 g)

INSTRUCTIONS

1. Fill the bread maker pan with all the ingredients in the order listed, starting with adding the liquids, followed by the dry components, ensuring the yeast is added last, on top of the flour.
2. Select the Basic/Whole Wheat Setting on the bread maker and choose the desired loaf size (1 pound, 1.5 pounds, or 2 pounds).
3. Start the bread maker. The process of mixing the ingredients will begin.
4. Let the dough rise in the bread maker for approximately 1 hour or until it reaches the top of the pan.
5. The bread maker will automatically start the baking cycle once the rising cycle is complete.
6. After the baking cycle, before slicing, cool on a wire rack when it has been removed from the pan.

NUTRITION PER SERVING (1 SLICE): CALORIES 120; FAT 3G; CARBS 18G; PROTEIN 5G; FIBER 1G; SODIUM 200MG

PEPPERONI AND PROVOLONE BREAD

PREP TIME: 10 MINUTES
RISING TIME: 1-2 HOURS
BAKING TIME: APPROXIMATELY 1 HOUR
COMPLEXITY: BEGINNER

TOOL FUNCTION:
BREAD MAKER OPERATING SETTING:
BASIC/WHOLE WHEAT SETTING
BAKING TEMPERATURE: 375°F (190°C)

TOOLS NEEDED:
BREAD MAKER
MEASURING CUPS AND SPOONS
KNIFE AND CUTTING BOARD

INGREDIENTS	1 POUND	1.5 POUND	2 POUND
WARM MILK	½ cup (120 ml)	¾ cup (180 ml)	1 cup (240 ml)
UNSALTED BUTTER	1 tbsp. (15 g)	1 ½ tbsps. (22.5 g)	2 tbsps. (30 g)
BREAD FLOUR	1 ½ cups (180 g)	2 ¼ cups (270 g)	3 cups (360 g)
GRANULATED SUGAR	½ tbsp. (7.5 g)	1 tbsp. (15 g)	1 tbsp. (15 g)
SALT	¾ tsp. (3.5 g)	1 ⅛ tsps. (5.25 g)	1 ½ tsps. (7 g)
SHREDDED PROVOLONE CHEESE	½ cup (75 g)	¾ cup (112.5 g)	1 cup (150 g)
CHOPPED PEPPERONI	¼ cup (30 g)	⅓ cup (40 g)	½ cup (60 g)
ACTIVE DRY YEAST	¾ tsp. (3.5 g)	1 ⅛ tsps. (5.25 g)	1 ½ tsps. (7 g)

INSTRUCTIONS

1. Fill the bread maker pan with all the ingredients in the order listed, starting with adding the liquids, followed by the dry components, ensuring the yeast is added last, on top of the flour.
2. Select the Basic/Whole Wheat Setting on the bread maker and choose the desired loaf size (1 pound, 1.5 pounds, or 2 pounds).
3. Start the bread maker. The process of mixing the ingredients will begin.
4. Let the dough rise in the bread maker for approximately 1 hour or until it reaches the top of the pan.
5. The bread maker will automatically start the baking cycle once the rising cycle is complete.
6. After the baking cycle, before slicing, cool on a wire rack when it has been removed from the pan.

NUTRITION PER SERVING (1 SLICE): CALORIES 130; FAT 5G; CARBS 15G; PROTEIN 6G; FIBER 1G; SODIUM 250MG

GRUYERE AND BACON BREAD

PREP TIME: 10 MINUTES
RISING TIME: 1-2 HOURS
BAKING TIME: APPROXIMATELY 1 HOUR
COMPLEXITY: BEGINNER

TOOL FUNCTION:
BREAD MAKER OPERATING SETTING:
BASIC/WHOLE WHEAT SETTING
BAKING TEMPERATURE: 375°F (190°C)

TOOLS NEEDED:
BREAD MAKER
MEASURING CUPS AND
SPOONS
KNIFE AND CUTTING BOARD

INGREDIENTS	1 POUND	1.5 POUND	2 POUND
WARM WATER	½ cup (120 ml)	¾ cup (180 ml)	1 cup (240 ml)
OLIVE OIL	1 tbsp. (15 g)	1 ½ tbsps. (22.5 g)	2 tbsps. (30 g)
BREAD FLOUR	1 ½ cups (180 g)	2 ¼ cups (270 g)	3 cups (360 g)
GRANULATED SUGAR	½ tbsp. (7.5 g)	1 tbsp. (15 g)	1 tbsp. (15 g)
SALT	¾ tsp. (3.5 g)	1 ⅛ tsps. (5.25 g)	1 ½ tsps. (7 g)
SHREDDED GRUYERE CHEESE	½ cup (75 g)	¾ cup (112.5 g)	1 cup (150 g)
COOKED AND CRUMBLED BACON	¼ cup (30 g)	⅓ cup (40 g)	½ cup (60 g)
ACTIVE DRY YEAST	¾ tsp. (3.5 g)	1 ⅛ tsps. (5.25 g)	1 ½ tsps. (7 g)

INSTRUCTIONS
1. Fill the bread maker pan with all the ingredients in the order listed, starting with adding the liquids, followed by the dry components, ensuring the yeast is added last, on top of the flour.
2. Select the Basic/Whole Wheat Setting on the bread maker and choose the desired loaf size (1 pound, 1.5 pounds, or 2 pounds).
3. Start the bread maker. The process of mixing the ingredients will begin.
4. Let the dough rise in the bread maker for approximately 1 hour or until it reaches the top of the pan.
5. The bread maker will automatically start the baking cycle once the rising cycle is complete.
6. After the baking cycle, before slicing, cool on a wire rack when it has been removed from the pan.

NUTRITION PER SERVING (1 SLICE): CALORIES 140; FAT 6G; CARBS 15G; PROTEIN 7G; FIBER 1G; SODIUM 250MG

CHEDDAR AND JALAPENO CORNBREAD

PREP TIME: 10 MINUTES
RISING TIME: 1-2 HOURS
BAKING TIME: APPROXIMATELY 1 HOUR
COMPLEXITY: BEGINNER

TOOL FUNCTION:
BREAD MAKER OPERATING SETTING:
BASIC/WHOLE WHEAT SETTING
BAKING TEMPERATURE: 375°F (190°C)

TOOLS NEEDED:
BREAD MAKER
MEASURING CUPS AND
SPOONS
KNIFE AND CUTTING BOARD

INGREDIENTS	1 POUND	1.5 POUND	2 POUND
WARM MILK	½ cup (120 ml)	¾ cup (180 ml)	1 cup (240 ml)
UNSALTED BUTTER (SOFTENED)	1 tbsp. (15 g)	1 ½ tbsps. (22.5 g)	2 tbsps. (30 g)
CORNMEAL	⅜ cup (60 g)	9/16 cup (90 g)	¾ cup (120 g)
BREAD FLOUR	1 cup (120 g)	1 ½ cups (180 g)	2 cups (240 g)
GRANULATED SUGAR	½ tbsp. (7.5 g)	½ tbsp. (7.5 g)	1 tbsp. (15 g)
SALT	¾ tsp. (3.5 g)	1 ⅛ tsps. (5.25 g)	1 ½ tsps. (7 g)
ACTIVE DRY YEAST	¾ tsp. (3.5 g)	1 ⅛ tsps. (5.25 g)	1 ½ tsps. (7 g)
SHREDDED CHEDDAR CHEESE	⅝ cup (75 g)	15/16 cup (112.5 g)	1 ¼ cups (150 g)
DICED PICKLED JALAPENOS	⅛ cup (15 g)	3/16 cup (22.5 g)	¼ cup (30 g)

INSTRUCTIONS
1. Fill the bread maker pan with all the ingredients in the order listed, starting with adding the liquids, followed by the dry components, ensuring the yeast is added last, on top of the flour.
2. Select the Basic/Whole Wheat Setting on the bread maker and choose the desired loaf size (1 pound, 1.5 pounds, or 2 pounds).
3. Start the bread maker. The process of mixing the ingredients will begin.
4. Let the dough rise in the bread maker for approximately 1 hour or until it reaches the top of the pan.
5. The bread maker will automatically start the baking cycle once the rising cycle is complete.
6. After the baking cycle, before slicing, cool on a wire rack when it has been removed from the pan.

NUTRITION PER SERVING (1 SLICE): CALORIES 120; FAT 4G; CARBS 18G; PROTEIN 5G; FIBER 1G; SODIUM 250MG

HAVARTI AND DILL BREAD

PREP TIME: 10 MINUTES
RISING TIME: 1-2 HOURS
BAKING TIME: APPROXIMATELY 1 HOUR
COMPLEXITY: BEGINNER

TOOL FUNCTION:
BREAD MAKER OPERATING SETTING:
BASIC/WHOLE WHEAT SETTING
BAKING TEMPERATURE: 375°F (190°C)

TOOLS NEEDED:
BREAD MAKER
MEASURING CUPS AND
SPOONS
KNIFE AND CUTTING BOARD

INGREDIENTS	1 POUND	1.5 POUND	2 POUND
WARM MILK	½ cup (120 ml)	¾ cup (180 ml)	1 cup (240 ml)
UNSALTED BUTTER (SOFTENED)	1 tbsp. (15 g)	1 ½ tbsps. (22.5 g)	2 tbsps. (30 g)
BREAD FLOUR	1 ½ cups (180 g)	2 ¼ cups (270 g)	3 cups (360 g)
GRANULATED SUGAR	½ tbsp. (7.5 g)	¾ tbsp. (11.25 g)	1 tbsp. (15 g)
SALT	¾ tsp. (3.5 g)	1 ⅛ tsps. (5.25 g)	1 ½ tsps. (7 g)
SHREDDED HAVARTI CHEESE	½ cup (75 g)	¾ cup (112.5 g)	1 cup (150 g)
CHOPPED FRESH DILL	1 tbsp. (4 g)	1 ½ tbsps. (6 g)	2 tbsps. (8 g)
ACTIVE DRY YEAST	¾ tsp. (3.5 g)	1 ⅛ tsps. (5.25 g)	1 ½ tsps. (7 g)

INSTRUCTIONS

1. Fill the bread maker pan with all the ingredients in the order listed, starting with adding the liquids, followed by the dry components, ensuring the yeast is added last, on top of the flour.
2. Select the Basic/Whole Wheat Setting on the bread maker and choose the desired loaf size (1 pound, 1.5 pounds, or 2 pounds).
3. Start the bread maker. The process of mixing the ingredients will begin.
4. Let the dough rise in the bread maker for approximately 1 hour or until it reaches the top of the pan.
5. The bread maker will automatically start the baking cycle once the rising cycle is complete.
6. After the baking cycle, before slicing, cool on a wire rack when it has been removed from the pan.

NUTRITION PER SERVING (1 SLICE): CALORIES 130; FAT 4G; CARBS 18G; PROTEIN 6G; FIBER 1G; SODIUM 230MG

GOUDA AND BACON BREAD

PREP TIME: 10 MINUTES
RISING TIME: 1-2 HOURS
BAKING TIME: APPROXIMATELY 1 HOUR
COMPLEXITY: BEGINNER

TOOL FUNCTION:
BREAD MAKER OPERATING SETTING:
BASIC/WHOLE WHEAT SETTING
BAKING TEMPERATURE: 375°F (190°C)

TOOLS NEEDED:
BREAD MAKER
MEASURING CUPS AND
SPOONS
KNIFE AND CUTTING BOARD

INGREDIENTS	1 POUND	1.5 POUND	2 POUND
WARM WATER	½ cup (120 ml)	¾ cup (180 ml)	1 cup (240 ml)
OLIVE OIL	1 tbsp. (15 g)	1 ½ tbsps. (22.5 g)	2 tbsps. (30 g)
BREAD FLOUR	1 ½ cups (180 g)	2 ¼ cups (270 g)	3 cups (360 g)
GRANULATED SUGAR	½ tbsp. (7.5 g)	¾ tbsp. (11.25 g)	1 tbsp. (15 g)
SALT	¾ tsp. (3.5 g)	1 ⅛ tsps. (5.25 g)	1 ½ tsps. (7 g)
SHREDDED GOUDA CHEESE	½ cup (75 g)	¾ cup (112.5 g)	1 cup (150 g)
COOKED AND CRUMBLED BACON	¼ cup (30 g)	⅓ cup (40 g)	½ cup (60 g)
ACTIVE DRY YEAST	¾ tsp. (3.5 g)	1 ⅛ tsps. (5.25 g)	1 ½ tsps. (7 g)

INSTRUCTIONS

1. Fill the bread maker pan with all the ingredients in the order listed, starting with adding the liquids, followed by the dry components, ensuring the yeast is added last, on top of the flour.
2. Select the Basic/Whole Wheat Setting on the bread maker and choose the desired loaf size (1 pound, 1.5 pounds, or 2 pounds).
3. Start the bread maker. The process of mixing the ingredients will begin.
4. Let the dough rise in the bread maker for approximately 1 hour or until it reaches the top of the pan.
5. The bread maker will automatically start the baking cycle once the rising cycle is complete.
6. After the baking cycle, before slicing, cool on a wire rack when it has been removed from the pan.

NUTRITION PER SERVING (1 SLICE): CALORIES 110; FAT 3G; CARBS 15G; PROTEIN 4G; FIBER 1G; SODIUM 200MG

SWEET BREAD

CLASSIC BANANA BREAD

PREP TIME: 10 MINUTES
RISING TIME: NONE
BAKING TIME: APPROXIMATELY 1 HOUR
COMPLEXITY: INTERMEDIATE

TOOL FUNCTION:
BREAD MAKER OPERATING SETTING:
BASIC/WHOLE WHEAT SETTING
BAKING TEMPERATURE: 375°F (190°C)

TOOLS NEEDED:
BREAD MAKER
MEASURING CUPS AND SPOONS
MIXING BOWL

INGREDIENTS	1 POUND	1.5 POUND	2 POUND
ALL-PURPOSE FLOUR	1 cup (120 g)	1 ½ cups (180 g)	2 cups (240 g)
BAKING SODA	½ tsp. (2.5 g)	¾ tsp. (3.75 g)	1 tsp. (5 g)
SALT	¼ tsp. (1.25 g)	⅜ tsp. (1.875 g)	½ tsp. (2.5 g)
UNSALTED BUTTER (MELTED)	¼ cup (57 g)	⅜ cup (86 g)	½ cup (115 g)
GRANULATED SUGAR	½ cup (100 g)	¾ cup (150 g)	1 cup (200 g)
LARGE EGGS	1	1	2
VANILLA EXTRACT	½ tsp. (2.5 ml)	¾ tsp. (3.75 ml)	1 tsp. (5 ml)
RIPE BANANAS (MASHED)	2	3	4

INSTRUCTIONS

1. Flour, baking soda, and salt should be mixed together in a mixing basin. Mix well.
2. Mix the melted butter and sugar in a separate bowl until well combined.
3. Combine the eggs and vanilla essence into the butter-sugar mixture and whisk until smooth.
4. Stir in the mashed bananas until evenly incorporated.
5. Gradually incorporate the dry ingredients into the wet mixture, stirring until combined.
6. Pour the batter into the bread maker pan, spreading it evenly.
7. Place the bread maker pan into the bread maker and select the desired loaf size (one pound, one and a half, or two pounds) and additionally the basic setting.
8. Start the bread maker and let it cycle, including mixing, kneading, rising, and baking.
9. Once the baking cycle is complete, carefully taking the bread out of the bread maker, transfer the pan to a wire tray to cool down before slicing and serving.

NUTRITION PER SERVING (1 SLICE): CALORIES 110; FAT 3G; CARBS 15G; PROTEIN 4G; FIBER 1G; SODIUM 200MG

CHOCOLATE ZUCCHINI BREAD

PREP TIME: 15 MINUTES
RISING TIME: 1-2 HOURS
BAKING TIME: APPROXIMATELY 1 HOUR
COMPLEXITY: INTERMEDIATE

TOOL FUNCTION:
BREAD MAKER OPERATING SETTING:
QUICK BREAD/CAKE SETTING
BAKING TEMPERATURE: 350°F (175°C)

TOOLS NEEDED:
BREAD MAKER
MEASURING CUPS AND
SPOONS
MIXING BOWL

INGREDIENTS	1 POUND	1.5 POUND	2 POUND
WARM WATER	¾ cup (180 ml)	1 cup (240 ml)	1 ⅓ cups (320 ml)
UNSALTED BUTTER (SOFTENED)	2 tbsps. (30 g)	3 tbsps. (45 g)	4 tbsps. (60 g)
BREAD FLOUR	1 ¾ cups (210 g)	2 ½ cups (300 g)	3 ⅓ cups (400 g)
GRANULATED SUGAR	2 tsps. (10 g)	1 tbsp. (15 g)	2 tbsps. (30 g)
SALT	½ tsp. (2.5 g)	¾ tsp. (3.75 g)	1 tsp. (5 g)
ACTIVE DRY YEAST	¾ tsp. (3 g)	1 tsp. (5 g)	1 ⅓ tsps. (6.67 g)
UNSWEETENED COCOA POWDER	¼ cup (25 g)	⅓ cup (35 g)	½ cup (55 g)
BAKING SODA	¼ tsp. (1.25 g)	⅓ tsp. (1.75 g)	½ tsp. (2.5 g)
BAKING POWDER	⅛ tsp. (0.625 g)	⅙ tsp. (0.833 g)	¼ tsp. (1.25 g)
UNSALTED BUTTER (SOFTENED)	¼ cup (55 g)	⅓ cup (75 g)	½ cup (110 g)
GRANULATED SUGAR	½ cup (100 g)	¾ cup (150 g)	1 cup (200 g)
EGG	1 large	1 large	1 large
VANILLA EXTRACT	½ tsp. (2.5 ml)	¾ tsp. (3.75 ml)	1 tsp. (5 ml)
MILK	¼ cup (60 ml)	⅓ cup (80 ml)	½ cup (120 ml)
GRATED ZUCCHINI	¾ cup (100 g)	1 cup (150 g)	1 ⅓ cups (200 g)
CHOCOLATE CHIPS	½ cup (87.5 g)	¾ cup (131.25 g)	1 cup (175 g)

INSTRUCTIONS

1. Place the warm water and softened butter into the bread machine pan.
2. Mix bread flour, sugar, salt, and yeast in a separate bowl. Put this mix in the bread machine pan.
3. Set the bread machine to "Quick Bread" or "Cake" setting to bypass unnecessary rising phases. Leave the dough there until it is well mixed and has risen adequately.
4. While the dough is mixing, prepare the chocolate mixture. Put cocoa powder, baking soda, and baking powder in a small bowl and mix them together.
5. In another bowl, cream softened butter and granulated sugar until airy and frothy. Integrate the vanilla essence and the egg into the mixture until thoroughly combined.
6. Gradually add the sifted cocoa mixture and milk to the combined mixture in turns until smooth.
7. Once the dough cycle is complete, remove the dough from the bread machine and gently fold in the chocolate mixture, grated zucchini, and chocolate chips until evenly distributed.
8. Grease the bread machine pan and transfer the dough into it, spreading it evenly.
9. Close the lid of the bread machine and select the "Quick Bread" or "Cake" cycle, depending on your machine's options.
10. Let the bread machine run through the cycle, including mixing and baking.
11. Once the cycle is complete, cut it into slices and serve.

- -

NUTRITION PER SERVING (1 SLICE): CALORIES 180; FAT 8G; CARBS 25G; PROTEIN 3G; FIBER 2G; SODIUM 200MG

APPLE CINNAMON BREAD

PREP TIME: 15 MINUTES
RISING TIME: 1-2 HOURS
BAKING TIME: APPROXIMATELY 1 HOUR
COMPLEXITY: BEGINNER

TOOL FUNCTION:
BREAD MAKER OPERATING SETTING: QUICK BREAD/CAKE SETTING BAKING TEMPERATURE: 350°F (175°C)

TOOLS NEEDED:
BREAD MAKER
MEASURING CUPS AND SPOONS
KNIFE AND CUTTING BOARD
MIXING BOWL

INGREDIENTS	1 POUND	1.5 POUND	2 POUND
WARM WATER	¾ cup (180 ml)	1 cup (240 ml)	1 ¼ cups (300 ml)
UNSALTED BUTTER (SOFTENED)	1 ½ tbsps. (22.5 g)	2 tbsps. (30 g)	2 ½ tbsps. (37.5 g)
BREAD FLOUR	2 ¼ cups (270 g)	3 cups (360 g)	4 cups (480 g)
GRANULATED SUGAR	¾ tbsp. (11 g)	1 ½ tbsps. (22.5 g)	2 tbsps. (30 g)
SALT	1 tsp. (5 g)	1 ½ tsps. (7 g)	1 ½ tsps. (7 g)
ACTIVE DRY YEAST	¾ tsp. (3 g)	1 ½ tsps. (7 g)	2 tsps. (10 g)
CHOPPED APPLES	¾ cup (75 g)	1 cup (100 g)	1 ¼ cups (125 g)
GROUND CINNAMON	¾ tsp. (3 g)	1 ½ tsps. (7 g)	2 tsps. (10 g)

INSTRUCTIONS

1. Place the warm water and softened butter into the bread machine pan.
2. Mix bread flour, sugar, salt, and yeast in a separate bowl. Incorporate this amalgamation into the bread machine pan.
3. Activate the dough cycle on the bread machine and let it operate until it is well mixed and has risen adequately.
4. Once the dough cycle is complete, gently fold the chopped apples and ground cinnamon until evenly distributed.
5. Grease the bread machine pan and transfer the dough into it, spreading it evenly.
6. Close the lid of the bread machine and select the "Quick Bread" or "Cake" cycle, depending on your machine's options.
7. Let the bread machine run through the cycle, including mixing and baking.
8. Once the cycle is complete, carefully remove the bread from the bread machine. Place the pan on a wire rack and allow it to cool prior to slicing and serving.

NUTRITION PER SERVING (1 SLICE): CALORIES 150; FAT 4G; CARBS 25G; PROTEIN 3G; FIBER 2G; SODIUM 200MG

BLUEBERRY LEMON BREAD

PREP TIME: 15 MINUTES
RISING TIME: 1-2 HOURS
BAKING TIME: APPROXIMATELY 1 HOUR
COMPLEXITY: BEGINNER

TOOL FUNCTION:
BREAD MAKER OPERATING SETTING: QUICK BREAD/CAKE SETTING BAKING TEMPERATURE: 350°F (175°C)

TOOLS NEEDED:
BREAD MAKER
MEASURING CUPS AND SPOONS
MIXING BOWL

INGREDIENTS	1 POUND	1.5 POUND	2 POUND
WARM WATER	¾ cup (180 ml)	1 cup (240 ml)	1 ¼ cups (300 ml)
UNSALTED BUTTER (SOFTENED)	1 ½ tbsps. (22.5 g)	2 tbsps. (30 g)	2 ½ tbsps. (37.5 g)
ZEST OF LEMON	Zest of 1 lemon	Zest of 1 lemon	Zest of 1 lemon
FRESH LEMON JUICE	¼ cup (60 ml)	¼ cup (60 ml)	¼ cup (60 ml)
MILK	¼ cup (60 ml)	¼ cup (60 ml)	¼ cup (60 ml)
BREAD FLOUR	2 ¼ cups (270 g)	3 cups (360 g)	4 cups (480 g)
GRANULATED SUGAR	¾ tbsp. (11 g)	1 ½ tbsps. (22.5 g)	2 tbsps. (30 g)
SALT	1 tsp. (5 g)	1 ½ tsps. (7 g)	1 ½ tsps. (7 g)
ACTIVE DRY YEAST	¾ tsp. (3 g)	1 ½ tsps. (7 g)	2 tsps. (10 g)
FRESH BLUEBERRIES	1 cup (150 g)	1 ½ cups (225 g)	2 cups (300 g)

INSTRUCTIONS

1. Place the warm water and softened butter into the bread machine pan.
2. Add the lemon zest, juice, and milk to the bread machine pan.
3. Combine bread flour, sugar, salt, and yeast in a separate bowl. Put this mix in the bread machine pan.
4. Set the bread machine to "dough" and leave it there until the dough is well mixed and has risen adequately.
5. Once the dough cycle is complete, carefully mix in the fresh blueberries until they are spread out evenly.
6. Grease the bread machine pan and transfer the dough into it, spreading it evenly.
7. Close the lid of the bread machine and select the "Quick Bread" or "Cake" cycle, depending on your machine's options.
8. Let the bread machine run through the cycle, including mixing and baking.
9. Once the cycle is complete, carefully cool the bread. Then cut it into slices and serve.

NUTRITION PER SERVING (1 SLICE): CALORIES 150; FAT 4G; CARBS 25G; PROTEIN 3G; FIBER 2G; SODIUM 200MG

CHOCOLATE CHERRY BRIOCHE

PREP TIME: 15 MINUTES
RISING TIME: 1-2 HOURS
BAKING TIME: APPROXIMATELY 1 HOUR
COMPLEXITY: INTERMEDIATE

TOOL FUNCTION:
BREAD MAKER OPERATING SETTING:
DOUGH/BASIC/WHITE BREAD SETTING
BAKING TEMPERATURE: 350°F (175°C)

TOOLS NEEDED:
BREAD MAKER
MEASURING CUPS AND SPOONS
KNIFE AND CUTTING BOARD

INGREDIENTS	1 POUND	1.5 POUND	2 POUND
WARM MILK	½ cup (120 ml)	¾ cup (180 ml)	1 cup (240 ml)
GRANULATED SUGAR	2 tbsps. (25 g)	3 tbsps. (37.5 g)	¼ cup (50 g)
ACTIVE DRY YEAST	1 ⅛ tsps. (3.5 g)	1 ½ tsps. (4.5 g)	2 ¼ tsps. (7 g)
ALL-PURPOSE FLOUR	1 ¾ cups (210 g)	2 ⅝ cups (315 g)	3 ½ cups (420 g)
SALT	½ tsp. (2.5 g)	¾ tsp. (3.75 g)	1 tsp. (5 g)
UNSALTED BUTTER (SOFTENED)	¼ cup (55 g)	⅓ cup (73.3 g)	½ cup (115 g)
EGG	1 large	1 large	2 large
VANILLA EXTRACT	½ tsp. (2.5 ml)	¾ tsp. (3.75 ml)	1 tsp. (5 ml)
CHOPPED DARK CHOCOLATE	¼ cup (42.5 g)	⅓ cup (57.5 g)	½ cup (85 g)
DRIED CHERRIES	¼ cup (37.5 g)	⅓ cup (50 g)	½ cup (75 g)

INSTRUCTIONS

1. Add warm milk, granulated sugar, active dry yeast, all-purpose flour, salt, softened unsalted butter, a large egg, and vanilla extract to the bread pan, adjusting ingredients according to the desired loaf size.
2. Pick the dough setting on your bread machine (Dough/Basic/White Bread Setting) and start the cycle.
3. After kneading the dough and completing the cycle, incorporate the chopped dark chocolate and dried cherries into the dough.
4. Restart rotation of the dough. Take the bread machine dough out after the second kneading cycle.
5. Make a loaf out of the dough and put it in a greased loaf pan, if necessary.
6. Put the dough in a warm spot for approximately thirty to forty-five minutes or until it has doubled, covered with a clean kitchen towel.
7. Take the dough out of the loaf pan and place it back into the bread machine when it has risen.
8. Select the bake setting on your bread machine and set the time according to the manufacturer's instructions for your desired loaf size.
9. After baking, carefully take the bread out of the bread machine, set it on a wire rack to cool for a few minutes before cutting.

NUTRITION PER SERVING (1 SLICE): CALORIES 180; FAT 8G; CARBS 25G; PROTEIN 3G; FIBER 2G; SODIUM 200MG

CINNAMON RAISIN SWIRL BREAD

PREP TIME: 10 MINUTES
RISING TIME: 1-2 HOURS
BAKING TIME: APPROXIMATELY 1 HOUR
COMPLEXITY: INTERMEDIATE

TOOL FUNCTION:
BREAD MAKER OPERATING SETTING:
DOUGH/BASIC/WHITE BREAD SETTING
BAKING TEMPERATURE: 350°F (175°C)

TOOLS NEEDED:
BREAD MAKER
MEASURING CUPS AND SPOONS
ROLLING PIN

INGREDIENTS	1 POUND	1.5 POUND	2 POUND
WARM MILK	½ cup (120 ml)	¾ cup (180 ml)	1 cup (240 ml)
GRANULATED SUGAR	2 tbsps. (25 g)	3 tbsps. (37.5 g)	¼ cup (50 g)
ACTIVE DRY YEAST	2 ¼ tsps. (7 g)	2 ¼ tsps. (7 g)	2 ¼ tsps. (7 g)
ALL-PURPOSE FLOUR	1 ¾ cups (210 g)	2 ⅝ cups (315 g)	3 ½ cups (420 g)
SALT	½ tsp. (2.5 g)	¾ tsp. (3.75 g)	1 tsp. (5 g)
UNSALTED BUTTER	¼ cup (55 g)	⅓ cup (73.3 g)	¼ cup (55 g)
LARGE EGG	1	1	1
VANILLA EXTRACT	½ tsp. (2.5 ml)	¾ tsp. (3.75 ml)	1 tsp. (5 ml)
RAISINS	¼ cup (50 g)	⅓ cup (65 g)	½ cup (100 g)
PACKED BROWN SUGAR	2 tbsps. (25 g)	3 tbsps. (37.5 g)	¼ cup (50 g)
GROUND CINNAMON	1 ½ tsps. (7.5 g)	2 ¼ tsps. (11.25 g)	1 tbsp. (15 g)

INSTRUCTIONS

1. Combine warm milk, granulated sugar, and active dry yeast in the bread machine pan. Let it sit for 5-10 minutes until frothy.
2. Add all-purpose flour, salt, softened unsalted butter, egg, and vanilla extract to the bread machine pan.
3. Start the cycle by selecting the dough setting on your bread machine.
4. Take the dough out of the bread machine once it is kneaded and the cycle is finished.
5. The dough is rolled into a rectangle shape onto a floured surface.
6. Mix packed brown sugar and ground cinnamon in a small bowl.
7. Spread the brown sugar-cinnamon mixture evenly over the dough. Sprinkle raisins over the sugar-cinnamon mixture.
8. Begin rolling the dough from the long side to form a log. Seal the edges.
9. Transfer the rolled dough back into the bread machine pan.
10. Close the lid and let the bread machine operate on the dough setting for 30 minutes to allow the dough to rise.
11. After rising, close the lid and let the bread machine operate on the bake setting according to the selected loaf size.
12. Once the baking cycle is complete, gently take the loaf out of the bread machine and set it on a wire rack to cool before cutting.

NUTRITION PER SERVING (1 SLICE): CALORIES 120; FAT 4G; CARBS 20G; PROTEIN 3G; FIBER 1G; SODIUM 100MG

APPLE STREUSEL BREAD

PREP TIME: 10 MINUTES
RISING TIME: 1-2 HOURS
BAKING TIME: APPROXIMATELY 1 HOUR
COMPLEXITY: INTERMEDIATE

TOOL FUNCTION:
BREAD MAKER OPERATING SETTING:
DOUGH/BASIC/WHITE BREAD SETTING
BAKING TEMPERATURE: 350°F (175°C)

TOOLS NEEDED:
BREAD MAKER
MEASURING CUPS AND SPOONS
SMALL BOWL

INGREDIENTS	1 POUND	1.5 POUND	2 POUND
WARM MILK	1 cup (240 ml)	1 ½ cups (360 ml)	2 cups (480 ml)
UNSALTED BUTTER	½ cup (115 g)	¾ cup (170 g)	1 cup (225 g)
GRANULATED SUGAR	¾ cup (150 g)	2 tbsps. + 1 cup (225 g)	1 ⅓ cups (300 g)
LARGE EGGS	2	3	4
VANILLA EXTRACT	1 tsp. (5 ml)	1 ½ tsps. (7.5 ml)	2 tsps. (10 ml)
ALL-PURPOSE FLOUR	1 ½ cups (180 g)	2 ¼ cups (270 g)	3 cups (360 g)
BAKING POWDER	1 tsp. (5 g)	1 ½ tsps. (7.5 g)	2 tsps. (10 g)
BAKING SODA	¼ tsp. (1.25 g)	⅜ tsp. (1.9 g)	½ tsp. (2.5 g)
SALT	½ tsp. (2.5 g)	¾ tsp. (3.75 g)	1 tsp. (5 g)
MILK	¼ cup (60 ml)	⅜ cup (90 ml)	½ cup (120 ml)
CHOPPED FRESH APPLES	1 cup (125g)	1 ½ cups (188g)	2 cups (250g)
ALL-PURPOSE FLOUR (FOR TOPPING)	¼ cup (30 g)	⅜ cup (45 g)	½ cup (60 g)
BROWN SUGAR (PACKED) (FOR TOPPING)	¼ cup (50 g)	⅜ cup (75 g)	½ cup (100 g)
GROUND CINNAMON (FOR TOPPING)	1 tsp. (5 g)	1 ½ tsps. (7.5 g)	2 tsps. (10 g)
MELTED UNSALTED BUTTER (FOR TOPPING)	2 tbsps. (30 g)	3 tbsps. (45 g)	4 tbsps. (60 g)

INSTRUCTIONS

1. Combine warm milk, softened unsalted butter, sugar, eggs, vanilla extract and chopped apples in the bread machine pan.
2. Add all-purpose flour, salt, baking powder, and baking soda to the pan.
3. Pour in the additional ¼ cup of milk.
4. Place the bread machine pan into the bread machine and select the basic setting.
5. Prepare the streusel topping while the bread is mixing and kneading. Combine the all-purpose flour, packed brown sugar, and ground cinnamon in a small basin. Drizzle melted unsalted butter over the mixture and mix until crumbly.
6. When the bread machine signals, sprinkle the streusel topping evenly over the bread dough.
7. Close the bread machine and let it continue with the baking cycle.
8. Once the baking cycle is complete, gently take the loaf out of the bread machine and set it on a wire rack to cool before cutting and serving.

NUTRITION PER SERVING (1 SLICE): CALORIES 240; FAT 12G; CARBS 32G; PROTEIN 4G; FIBER 2G; SODIUM 180MG

LEMON POUND CAKE BREAD

PREP TIME: 10 MINUTES
RISING TIME: 1-2 HOURS
BAKING TIME: APPROXIMATELY 1 HOUR
COMPLEXITY: INTERMEDIATE

TOOL FUNCTION:
BREAD MAKER OPERATING SETTING:
CAKE/SWEET BREAD
BAKING TEMPERATURE: 350°F (175°C)

TOOLS NEEDED: BREAD MAKER
MEASURING CUPS
AND SPOONSWHISK

INGREDIENTS	1 POUND	1.5 POUND	2 POUND
ALL-PURPOSE FLOUR	¾ cup (90 g)	1 ⅛ cups (135 g)	1 ½ cups (180 g)
BAKING POWDER	½ tsp. (2.5 g)	¾ tsp. (3.75 g)	1 tsp. (5 g)
BAKING SODA	⅛ tsp. (0.625 g)	3/16 tsp. (0.938 g)	¼ tsp. (1.25 g)
SALT	¼ tsp. (1.25 g)	⅜ tsp. (1.875 g)	½ tsp. (2.5 g)
LEMON ZEST	Zest of ½ lemon	Zest of ¾ lemon	Zest of 1 lemon
UNSALTED BUTTER	¼ cup (57.5 g)	⅜ cup (86.25 g)	½ cup (115 g)
GRANULATED SUGAR	⅜ cup (75 g)	9/16 cup (112.5 g)	¾ cup (150 g)
LARGE EGG	1	1	2
VANILLA EXTRACT	½ tsp. (2.5 ml)	¾ tsp. (3.75 ml)	1 tsp. (5 ml)
FRESH LEMON JUICE	⅛ cup (30 ml)	3/16 cup (45 ml)	¼ cup (60 ml)
MILK	⅛ cup (30 ml)	3/16 cup (45 ml)	¼ cup (60 ml)
POWDERED SUGAR (FOR GLAZE)	½ cup (60 g)	¾ cup (90 g)	1 cup (120 g)
FRESH LEMON JUICE (FOR GLAZE)	1 tbsp. (15 ml)	1 ½ tbsps. (22.5 ml)	2 tbsps. (30 ml)

INSTRUCTIONS

1. Combine the baking powder, spice, salt, baking soda, flour, and zest of one lemon in the bread machine pan.
2. Add the softened unsalted butter, granulated sugar, egg(s), vanilla extract, lemon juice, and milk to baking pan in accordance with the directions on the specific measurements for the chosen loaf size.
3. Select the "Cake" or "Sweet Bread" setting on your bread maker, and begin the cycle.
4. Concurrently, compose the varnish by combining the fresh lemon juice and granulated sugar in a bowl and whisking them until they are very smooth. Set aside.
5. Once the bread machine cycle is complete, while the bread cools, carefully remove it from the pan and set it on a wire rack for a few minutes.
6. Drizzle the glaze over the warm bread, allowing it to soak in slightly.
7. Slice and serve the Lemon Pound Cake Bread, and enjoy its delightful citrus flavor!
8. Store any leftovers in a container that is airtight and kept at room temperature for up to three days.

- -

NUTRITION PER SERVING (1 SLICE): CALORIES 220; FAT 5G; CARBS 29G; PROTEIN 4G; FIBER 1G; SODIUM 200MG

PINEAPPLE COCONUT BREAD

PREP TIME: 10 MINUTES
RISING TIME: 1-2 HOURS
BAKING TIME: APPROXIMATELY 1 HOUR
COMPLEXITY: BEGINNER

TOOL FUNCTION:
BREAD MAKER OPERATING SETTING:
QUICK BREAD/CAKE SETTING
BAKING TEMPERATURE: 350°F (175°C)

TOOLS NEEDED: BREAD MAKER
MEASURING CUPS AND SPOONS
KNIFE AND CUTTING BOARD
MIXING BOWL

INGREDIENTS	1 POUND	1.5 POUND	2 POUND
ALL-PURPOSE FLOUR	¾ cup (90 g)	1 ⅛ cups (135 g)	1 ½ cups (180 g)
BAKING POWDER	1 tsp. (5 g)	1 ½ tsps. (7.5 g)	2 tsps. (10 g)
BAKING SODA	¼ tsp. (1.25 g)	⅜ tsp. (1.875 g)	½ tsp. (2.5 g)
SALT	½ tsp. (2.5 g)	¾ tsp. (3.75 g)	1 tsp. (5 g)
UNSALTED BUTTER	¼ cup (57.5 g)	¼ cup (57.5 g)	½ cup (115 g)
GRANULATED SUGAR	⅜ cup (75 g)	9/16 cup (112.5 g)	¾ cup (150 g)
LARGE EGG	1	1	2
VANILLA EXTRACT	½ tsp. (2.5 ml)	¾ tsp. (3.75 ml)	1 tsp. (5 ml)
PINEAPPLE JUICE	2 tbsps. (30 ml)	3 tbsps. (45 ml)	¼ cup (60 ml)
SHREDDED COCONUT	¼ cup (30 g)	⅜ cup (45 g)	½ cup (60 g)

INSTRUCTIONS

1. Combine warm milk, softened unsalted butter, granulated sugar, eggs, and vanilla extract in the bread Mix the all-purpose flour, baking powder, baking soda, and salt in a bowl that is suitable for mixing.
2. Unsalted butter that has been melted and granulated sugar should be creamed in a separate bowl until the mixture is frothy and light.
3. Using a mixer, incorporate the egg and vanilla extract until well combined.
4. To the creamed mixture, gradually incorporate the dry ingredients, alternating with the pineapple juice, until well combined.
5. Gently fold in the shredded coconut until evenly distributed throughout the batter.
6. Grease the bread machine pan and pour the batter into it, spreading it evenly.
7. Close the lid of the bread machine and select the "Quick Bread" or "Cake" cycle, depending on your machine's options.
8. Let the bread machine run through the cycle, including mixing and baking.
9. Once the cycle is complete, gently remove the bread from the bread machine pan, placing it on a wire rack to chill before slicing it and serving.

NUTRITION PER SERVING (1 SLICE): CALORIES 160; FAT 3G; CARBS 22G; PROTEIN 4G; FIBER 1G; SODIUM 180MG

APRICOT ALMOND BREAD

PREP TIME: 10 MINUTES
RISING TIME: 1-2 HOURS
BAKING TIME: APPROXIMATELY 1 HOUR
COMPLEXITY: BEGINNER

TOOL FUNCTION:
BREAD MAKER OPERATING SETTING: QUICK
BREAD/CAKE SETTING
BAKING TEMPERATURE: 350°F (175°C)

TOOLS NEEDED: BREAD MAKER
MEASURING CUPS AND SPOONS
KNIFE AND CUTTING BOARD
MIXING BOWL

INGREDIENTS	1 POUND	1.5 POUND	2 POUND
ALL-PURPOSE FLOUR	¾ cup (90 g)	1 ⅛ cups (135 g)	1 ½ cups (180 g)
BAKING POWDER	1 tsp. (5 g)	1 ½ tsps. (7.5 g)	2 tsps. (10 g)
BAKING SODA	¼ tsp. (1.25 g)	⅜ tsp. (1.875 g)	½ tsp. (2.5 g)
SALT	½ tsp. (2.5 g)	¾ tsp. (3.75 g)	1 tsp. (5 g)
CHOPPED ALMONDS	¼ cup (50 g)	⅜ cup (86.25 g)	½ cup (115 g)
UNSALTED BUTTER	¼ cup (57.5 g)	⅜ cup (86.25 g)	½ cup (115 g)
GRANULATED SUGAR	⅜ cup (75 g)	9/16 cup (112.5 g)	¾ cup (150 g)
LARGE EGG	1	1	2
ALMOND EXTRACT	½ tsp. (2.5 ml)	¾ tsp. (3.75 ml)	1 tsp. (5 ml)
MILK	⅛ cup (30 ml)	3 tbsps. (45 ml)	¼ cup (60 ml)
CHOPPED DRIED APRICOTS	½ cup (75 g)	¾ cup (112.5 g)	1 cup (150 g)

INSTRUCTIONS

1. Mix the all-purpose flour, baking powder, baking soda, and salt in a bowl that is suitable for mixing. Add the chopped almonds and mix well.
2. Unsalted butter that has been melted and granulated sugar should be creamed together in a separate bowl until the mixture is frothy and light.
3. The egg and almond essence should be beaten in until well combined.
4. Combine the dry ingredients with the mixture that has been creamed gradually, alternating with the milk until everything is together.
5. Gently fold the chopped dried apricots until evenly distributed throughout the batter.
6. Grease the bread machine pan, pour the batter into it, and spread it evenly.
7. Close the lid of the bread machine and select the "Quick Bread" or "Cake" cycle, depending on your machine's options.
8. Let the bread machine run through the cycle, including mixing and baking.
9. Once the cycle is complete, gently remove the bread from the bread machine pan, placing it on a wire rack to chill before slicing it and serving.

NUTRITION PER SERVING (1 SLICE): CALORIES 150; FAT 3G; CARBS 25G; PROTEIN 2G; FIBER 1G; SODIUM 180MG

CRANBERRY WALNUT BREAD

PREP TIME: 10 MINUTES
RISING TIME: 1-2 HOURS
BAKING TIME: APPROXIMATELY 1 HOUR
COMPLEXITY: BEGINNER

TOOL FUNCTION:
BREAD MAKER OPERATING SETTING: QUICK
BREAD/CAKE SETTING
BAKING TEMPERATURE: 350°F (175°C)

TOOLS NEEDED: BREAD MAKER
MEASURING CUPS AND SPOONS
KNIFE AND CUTTING BOARD
MIXING BOWL

INGREDIENTS	1 POUND	1.5 POUND	2 POUND
ALL-PURPOSE FLOUR	¾ cup (90 g)	1 ⅛ cups (135 g)	1 ½ cups (180 g)
BAKING POWDER	1 tsp. (5 g)	1 ½ tsps. (7.5 g)	2 tsps. (10 g)
BAKING SODA	¼ tsp. (1.25 g)	⅜ tsp. (1.875 g)	½ tsp. (2.5 g)
SALT	½ tsp. (2.5 g)	¾ tsp. (3.75 g)	1 tsp. (5 g)
CHOPPED WALNUTS	½ cup (50 g)	¾ cup (75 g)	1 cup (100 g)
UNSALTED BUTTER	¼ cup (57.5 g)	⅜ cup (86.25 g)	½ cup (115 g)
GRANULATED SUGAR	⅜ cup (75 g)	9/16 cup (112.5 g)	¾ cup (150 g)
LARGE EGG	1	1	2
VANILLA EXTRACT	½ tsp. (2.5 ml)	¾ tsp. (3.75 ml)	1 tsp. (5 ml)
ORANGE JUICE	⅛ cup (30 ml)	3 tbsps. (45 ml)	¼ cup (60 ml)
DRIED CRANBERRIES	½ cup (50 g)	¾ cup (75 g)	1 cup (100 g)

INSTRUCTIONS

1. Mix the all-purpose flour, baking powder, baking soda, and salt in a bowl that is suitable for mixing. Add the chopped walnuts and mix well.
2. Unsalted butter that has been melted and granulated sugar should be creamed in a separate bowl until the mixture is frothy and light.
3. The egg and vanilla essence should be beaten in until well combined.
4. To the creamed mixture, gradually incorporate the dry ingredients with the citrus juice until well combined.
5. Gently fold the dried cranberries until evenly distributed throughout the batter.
6. Grease the bread machine pan and pour the batter into it, spreading it evenly.
7. Close the lid of the bread machine and select the "Quick Bread" or "Cake" cycle, depending on your machine's options.
8. Let the bread machine run through the cycle, including mixing and baking.
9. Once the cycle is complete, gently remove the bread from the bread machine pan, placing it on a wire rack to chill before slicing it and serving.

NUTRITION PER SERVING (1 SLICE): CALORIES 170; FAT 3G; CARBS 25G; PROTEIN 4G; FIBER 1G; SODIUM 180MG

MAPLE PECAN BREAD

PREP TIME: 10 MINUTES
RISING TIME: 1-2 HOURS
BAKING TIME: APPROXIMATELY 1 HOUR
COMPLEXITY: BEGINNER

TOOL FUNCTION:
BREAD MAKER OPERATING SETTING:
QUICK BREAD/CAKE SETTING
BAKING TEMPERATURE: 350°F (175°C)

TOOLS NEEDED: BREAD MAKER
MEASURING CUPS AND SPOONS
KNIFE AND CUTTING BOARD
MIXING BOWL

INGREDIENTS	1 POUND	1.5 POUND	2 POUND
ALL-PURPOSE FLOUR	¾ cup (90 g)	1 ⅛ cups (135 g)	1 ½ cups (180 g)
BAKING POWDER	1 tsp. (5 g)	1 ½ tsps. (7.5 g)	2 tsps. (10 g)
BAKING SODA	¼ tsp. (1.25 g)	⅜ tsp. (1.875 g)	½ tsp. (2.5 g)
SALT	½ tsp. (2.5 g)	¾ tsp. (3.75 g)	1 tsp. (5 g)
UNSALTED BUTTER	¼ cup (57.5 g)	¼ cup (57.5 g)	½ cup (115 g)
GRANULATED SUGAR	⅜ cup (75 g)	9/16 cup (112.5 g)	¾ cup (150 g)
LARGE EGG	1	1	2
VANILLA EXTRACT	½ tsp. (2.5 ml)	¾ tsp. (3.75 ml)	1 tsp. (5 ml)
MAPLE SYRUP	2 tbsps. (30 ml)	3 tbsps. (45 ml)	¼ cup (60 ml)
CHOPPED PECANS	¼ cup (30 g)	⅜ cup (45 g)	½ cup (60 g)

INSTRUCTIONS

1. Mix the all-purpose flour, baking powder, baking soda, and salt in a bowl that is suitable for mixing.
2. Unsalted butter that has been melted and granulated sugar should be creamed together in a separate bowl until the mixture is frothy and light.
3. Beat in the egg, vanilla extract, and maple syrup until well combined.
4. To the creamed mixture, gradually incorporate the dry ingredients until well combined.
5. Gently fold in the chopped pecans until evenly distributed throughout the batter.
6. Grease the bread machine pan and pour the batter into it, spreading it evenly.
7. Close the lid of the bread machine and select the "Quick Bread" or "Cake" cycle, depending on your machine's options.
8. Let the bread machine run through the cycle, including mixing and baking.
9. Once the cycle is complete, carefully remove the bread from the bread machine pan. Moreover, before slicing and serving it, allow it to cool on a wire rack.

NUTRITION PER SERVING (1 SLICE): CALORIES 160; FAT 5G; CARBS 20G; PROTEIN 4G; FIBER 1G; SODIUM 200MG

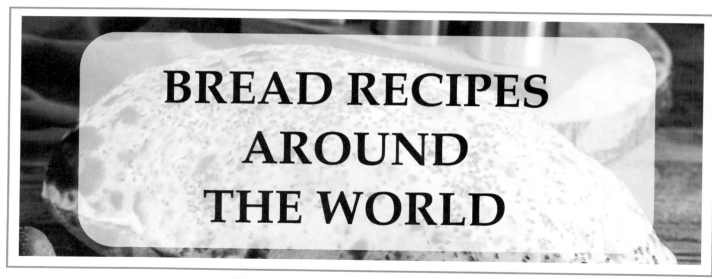

BREAD RECIPES AROUND THE WORLD

SWEDISH LIMPA BREAD

PREP TIME: 15 MINUTES
RISING TIME: 1 HOUR
BAKING TIME: APPROXIMATELY 1 HOUR
COMPLEXITY: BEGINNER

TOOL FUNCTION:
BREAD MAKER OPERATING SETTING:
BASIC/WHITE SETTING
BAKING TEMPERATURE: 375°F (190°C)

TOOLS NEEDED:
BREAD MAKER
MEASURING CUPS AND SPOONS
GRATER FOR ORANGE ZEST

INGREDIENTS	1 POUND	1.5 POUND	2 POUND
RYE FLOUR	¾ cup (90 g)	1 cup (120 g)	1 ½ cups (180 g)
BREAD FLOUR	½ cup (60 g)	¾ cup (90 g)	1 ⅛ cups (135 g)
SALT	½ tsp. (2.5 g)	¾ tsp. (3.75 g)	1 ⅛ tsp. (5.63 g)
ACTIVE DRY YEAST	½ tsp. (6 g)	¾ tsp. (9 g)	1 ⅛ tsp. (13.5 g)
MOLASSES	½ tsp. (7.5 g)	¾ tsp. (11.25 g)	1 ⅛ tsp. (16.88 g)
BROWN SUGAR	½ tsp. (7.5 g)	¾ tsp. (11.25 g)	1 ⅛ tsp. (16.88 g)
BUTTER	½ tsp. (7.5 g)	¾ tsp. (11.25 g)	1 ⅛ tsp. (16.88 g)
WARM WATER	½ cup (120 ml)	¾ cup (180 ml)	1 ½ cups (360 ml)
ORANGE JUICE	¼ cup (60 ml)	⅓ cup (80 ml)	½ cup (120 ml)
GRATED ORANGE ZEST	½ tbsp. (7.5 g)	¾ tbsp. (11.25 g)	1 ⅛ tbsp. (16.88 g)
FENNEL SEEDS	½ tsp. (2.5 g)	¾ tsp. (3.75 g)	1 ⅛ tsp. (5.63 g)

INSTRUCTIONS

1. Before using the bread maker pan, add all of the ingredients in the order listed, starting with the liquids, followed by the addition of the substances that are dry, ensuring the yeast is added last, on top of the flour.
2. Select the Basic/White Bread setting on the bread maker and choose the desired loaf size (1 pound, 1.5 pounds, or 2 pounds).
3. Start the bread maker. The process of mixing the ingredients will begin.
4. Let the dough rise in the bread maker for approximately 1 hour or until it reaches the top of the pan.
5. The bread maker will automatically start the baking cycle once the rising cycle is complete.
6. After the baking cycle, when you are ready to slice the bread, carefully remove it from the pan to a wire tray to cool.

NUTRITION PER SERVING (1 SLICE): : CALORIES 80; FAT 2G; CARBS 18G; PROTEIN 3G; FIBER 3G; SODIUM 150MG

PORTUGUESE BROA DE MILHO

PREP TIME: 15 MINUTES
RISING TIME: 1 HOUR
BAKING TIME: APPROXIMATELY 1 HOUR
COMPLEXITY: INTERMEDIATE

TOOL FUNCTION:
BREAD MAKER OPERATING SETTING:
BASIC/WHITE BREAD SETTING
BAKING TEMPERATURE: 375°F (190°C)

TOOLS NEEDED:
BREAD MAKER
MEASURING CUPS AND
SPOONS

INGREDIENTS	1 POUND	1.5 POUND	2 POUND
CORNMEAL	¾ cup (90 g)	1 ⅛ cups (135 g)	1 ½ cups (180 g)
ALL-PURPOSE FLOUR	⅜ cup (45 g)	9/16 cup (67.5 g)	¾ cup (90 g)
SALT	¼ tsp. (1.25 g)	⅜ tsp. (1.88 g)	½ tsp. (2.5 g)
ACTIVE DRY YEAST	⅜ tbsp. (4.5 g)	9/16 tbsp. (6.75 g)	¾ tbsp. (9 g)
WARM WATER	⅜ cup (90 ml)	9/16 cup (135 ml)	¾ cup (180 ml)
OLIVE OIL	¾ tbsp. (11.25 ml)	1 ⅛ tbsps. (16.88 ml)	1 ½ tbsps. (22.5 ml)

INSTRUCTIONS

1. Before using the bread maker pan, add all of the ingredients in the order listed, starting with the liquids, followed by the addition of the substances that are dry, ensuring the yeast is added last, on top of the flour.
2. On the bread maker, select the Basic/White Bread setting and choose the desired loaf size (1 pound, 1.5 pounds, or 2 pounds).
3. Start the bread maker. The process of mixing the ingredients will begin.
4. Let the dough rise in the bread maker for approximately 1 hour or until it reaches the top of the pan.
5. The bread maker will automatically start the baking cycle once the rising cycle is complete.
6. After the baking cycle, when you are ready to slice the bread, carefully remove it from the pan to a wire tray to cool.

NUTRITION PER SERVING (1 SLICE): CALORIES 120; FAT 2G; CARBS 22G; PROTEIN 3G; FIBER 3G; SODIUM 150MG

ONION RYE BREAD (GERMANY)

PREP TIME: 15 MINUTES
RISING TIME: 1 HOUR
BAKING TIME: APPROXIMATELY 1 HOUR
COMPLEXITY: INTERMEDIATE

TOOL FUNCTION:
BREAD MAKER OPERATING
SETTING: BASIC/ WHOLE WHEAT
SETTING BAKING TEMPERATURE:
375°F (190°C)

TOOLS NEEDED:
BREAD MAKER
MEASURING CUPS AND SPOONS
KNIFE AND CUTTING BOARD

INGREDIENTS	1 POUND	1.5 POUND	2 POUND
RYE FLOUR	¾ cup (90 g)	1 cup (120 g)	1 ½ cups (180 g)
BREAD FLOUR	½ cup (60 g)	¾ cup (90 g)	1 ⅛ cups (135 g)
CARAWAY SEEDS	½ tbsp. (6 g)	¾ tbsp. (9 g)	1 ½ tbsps. (18 g)
SALT	½ tsp. (2.5 g)	¾ tsp. (3.75 g)	1 tsp. (5 g)
ACTIVE DRY YEAST	¾ tsp. (3.5 g)	1 tsp. (5 g)	1 ½ tsps. (7.5 g)
BROWN SUGAR	½ tbsp. (7.5 g)	¾ tbsp. (11.25 g)	1 ½ tbsps. (22.5 g)
WARM WATER	¼ cup (60 ml)	⅓ cup (80 ml)	½ cup (120 ml)
BUTTERMILK	¼ cup (60 ml)	⅓ cup (80 ml)	½ cup (120 ml)
CHOPPED ONIONS	2 tbsps. (30 g)	3 tbsps. (45 g)	¼ cup (60 g)

INSTRUCTIONS

1. Measure all the ingredients according to the size of the bread you're making. Chop the onions finely.
2. Add the ingredients into the bread maker pan in the order listed in the ingredients list, starting with the liquids and then adding the dry ingredients.
3. Choose the appropriate bread size setting on your bread maker (1 pound, 1.5 pounds, or 2 pounds) and select the Basic/ Whole Wheat setting.
4. Ensure that the bread maker's lid is closed and start the machine. It should be allowed to go through the periods of kneading, rising, and baking.
5. When the baking cycle is complete, it is necessary to carefully remove the bread pan from the machine and check it for doneness. When tapped on the bottom it should sound hollow.
6. Let the bread cool for ten minutes in the pan, after which it should be shifted to a wire rack in order to complete chilling before slicing.

NUTRITION PER SERVING (1 SLICE): CALORIES 100; FAT 2G; CARBS 20G; PROTEIN 3G; FIBER 3G; SODIUM 150MG

SUNFLOWER SEED BREAD

PREP TIME: 10 MINUTES
RISING TIME: 1-2 HOURS
BAKING TIME: APPROXIMATELY 1 HOUR
COMPLEXITY: BEGINNER

TOOL FUNCTION:
BREAD MAKER OPERATING SETTING:
BASIC/ WHITE BREAD SETTING BAKING
TEMPERATURE: 375°F (190°C)

TOOLS NEEDED:
BREAD MAKER
MEASURING CUPS AND
SPOONS

INGREDIENTS	1 POUND	1.5 POUND	2 POUND
BREAD FLOUR	1 cup (120 g)	1.5 cups (180 g)	2 cups (240 g)
ACTIVE DRY YEAST	¾ tsp. (3.5 g)	1 tsp. (5 g)	1 ½ tsps. (7 g)
SALT	¾ tsp. (3.5 g)	1 tsp. (5 g)	1 ½ tsps. (7 g)
GRANULATED SUGAR	2 tbsps. (25 g)	3 tbsps. (37.5 g)	¼ cup (50 g)
VEGETABLE OIL	2 tbsps. (30 ml)	3 tbsps. (45 ml)	¼ cup (60 ml)
WARM WATER	⅝ cup (150 ml)	15/16 cup (225 ml)	1 ¼ cups (300 ml)
SUNFLOWER SEEDS	¼ cup (37.5 g)	⅜ cup (56.25 g)	½ cup (75 g)

INSTRUCTIONS

1. Before using the bread maker pan, add all of the ingredients in the order listed, starting with the liquids, followed by the addition of the substances that are dry, ensuring the yeast is added last, on top of the flour.
2. Select the Basic/White Bread setting on the bread maker and choose the desired loaf size (1 pound, 1.5 pounds, or 2 pounds).
3. Start the bread maker. The process of mixing the ingredients will begin.
4. Let the dough rise in the bread maker for approximately 1 hour or until it reaches the top of the pan.
5. The bread maker will automatically start the baking cycle once the rising cycle is complete.
6. After the baking cycle, when you are ready to slice the bread, carefully remove the pan and set aside to cool on a wire rack.

NUTRITION PER SERVING (1 SLICE): CALORIES 120; FAT 7G; CARBS 21G; PROTEIN 3G; FIBER 1G; SODIUM 220MG

FINNISH PULLA

PREP TIME: 10 MINUTES
RISING TIME: 1-2 HOURS
BAKING TIME: APPROXIMATELY 1 HOUR
COMPLEXITY: BEGINNER

TOOL FUNCTION:
BREAD MAKER OPERATING SETTING:
BASIC/WHITE BREAD SETTING
BAKING TEMPERATURE: 375°F (190°C)

TOOLS NEEDED:
BREAD MAKER
MEASURING CUPS AND SPOONS

INGREDIENTS	1 POUND	1.5 POUND	2 POUND
ALL-PURPOSE FLOUR	1 cup (120 g)	1.5 cups (180 g)	2 cups (240 g)
GRANULATED SUGAR	2 tbsps. (25 g)	3 tbsps. (37.5 g)	¼ cup (50 g)
SALT	½ tsp. (2.5 g)	¾ tsp. (3.75 g)	1 tsp. (5 g)
ACTIVE DRY YEAST	1 tsp. (5 g)	1.5 tsps. (7.5 g)	1 tbsp. (15 g)
WARM MILK	½ cup (120 ml)	¾ cup (180 ml)	1 cup (240 ml)
MELTED BUTTER	2 tbsps. (30 ml)	3 tbsps. (45 ml)	¼ cup (60 ml)
BEATEN EGG	¼ beaten egg	¼ beaten egg	½ beaten egg
GROUND CARDAMOM	¼ tsp. (1.25 ml)	⅜ tsp. (1.875 ml)	½ tsp. (2.5 ml)

INSTRUCTIONS

1. Before using the bread maker pan, add all of the ingredients in the order listed for the desired loaf size.
2. Select the bread maker`s Basic/White Bread setting with a stirring function.
3. Start the bread maker.
4. Let the bread maker run through its cycle, which typically takes about 3 hours. The bread machine will mix, knead, and proof the dough.
5. Once the mixing and kneading cycle is complete, allow the dough to rise in the bread maker until doubled in size.
6. If the dough has risen, use a spatula to deflate it gently.
7. Ensure that the bread maker's lid is close, and then allow it to continue with the baking cycle.
8. Once the baking cycle is complete, remove it from the bread maker and place it on a wire rack to cool.
9. Once cooled, slice the Finnish Pulla and serve.

NUTRITION PER SERVING (1 SLICE): CALORIES 130; FAT 5G; CARBS 21G; PROTEIN 2G; FIBER 1G; SODIUM 200MG

LITHUANIAN BREAD

PREP TIME: 10 MINUTES
RISING TIME: 1-2 HOURS
BAKING TIME: APPROXIMATELY 1 HOUR
COMPLEXITY: BEGINNER

TOOL FUNCTION:
BREAD MAKER OPERATING SETTING:
BASIC/ WHITE BREAD SETTING BAKING
TEMPERATURE: 375°F (190°C)

TOOLS NEEDED:
BREAD MAKER
MEASURING CUPS AND
SPOONS

INGREDIENTS	1 POUND	1.5 POUND	2 POUND
RYE FLOUR	1 cup (120 g)	1.5 cups (180 g)	2 cups (240 g)
BREAD FLOUR	2 cups (240 g)	3 cups (360 g)	4 cups (480 g)
BROWN SUGAR	1 tbsp. (15 g)	1.5 tbsps. (22.5 g)	2 tbsps. (30 g)
SALT	1 tsp. (5 g)	1.5 tsps. (7.5 g)	2 tsps. (10 g)
ACTIVE DRY YEAST	1 tbsp. (15 g)	1.5 tbsps. (22.5 g)	2 tbsps. (30 g)
WARM WATER	1 cup (240 ml)	1.5 cups (360 ml)	2 cups (480 ml)
MOLASSES	2 tbsps. (30 ml)	3 tbsps. (45 ml)	¼ cup (60 ml)
VEGETABLE OIL	1 tbsp. (15 ml)	1.5 tbsps. (22.5 ml)	2 tbsps. (30 ml)

INSTRUCTIONS

1. Before using the bread maker pan, add all of the ingredients in the order listed, starting with the liquids, followed by the addition of the substances that are dry, ensuring the yeast is added last, on top of the flour.
2. Select the Basic/White Bread setting on the bread maker and choose the desired loaf size (1 pound, 1.5 pounds, or 2 pounds).
3. Start the bread maker. The process of mixing the ingredients will begin.
4. Let the dough rise in the bread maker for approximately 1 hour or until it reaches the top of the pan.
5. The bread maker will automatically start the baking cycle once the rising cycle is complete.
6. After the baking cycle, when you are ready to slice the bread, carefully remove the pan and set aside to cool on a wire rack.

NUTRITION PER SERVING (1 SLICE): CALORIES 120; FAT 3G; CARBS 20G; PROTEIN 2G; FIBER 1G; SODIUM 230MG

ESTONIAN BREAD (LEIB)

PREP TIME: 10 MINUTES
RISING TIME: 1-2 HOURS
BAKING TIME: APPROXIMATELY 1 HOUR
COMPLEXITY: BEGINNER

TOOL FUNCTION:
BREAD MAKER OPERATING SETTING: WHOLE WHEAT BREAD SETTING
BAKING TEMPERATURE: 375°F (190°C)

TOOLS NEEDED:
BREAD MAKER
MEASURING CUPS AND SPOONS

INGREDIENTS	1 POUND	1.5 POUND	2 POUND
RYE FLOUR	1 cup (120 g)	1.5 cups (180 g)	2 cups (240 g)
WHOLE WHEAT FLOUR	1 cup (120 g)	1.5 cups (180 g)	2 cups (240 g)
DARK MOLASSES OR HONEY	1 tbsp. (15 g)	1.5 tbsps. (22.5 g)	2 tbsps. (30 g)
SALT	1 tsp. (5 g)	1.5 tsps. (7.5 g)	2 tsps. (10 g)
ACTIVE DRY YEAST	1 tbsp. (15 g)	1.5 tbsps. (22.5 g)	2 tbsps. (30 g)
WARM WATER	½ cup (120 ml)	¾ cup (180 ml)	1 cup (240 ml)
BUTTERMILK	½ cup (120 ml)	¾ cup (180 ml)	1 cup (240 ml)
VEGETABLE OIL	1 tbsp. (15 ml)	1.5 tbsps. (22.5 ml)	2 tbsps. (30 ml)
CARAWAY SEEDS	1 tbsp. (15 g)	1.5 tbsps. (22.5 g)	2 tbsps. (30 g)

INSTRUCTIONS

1. Add the warm water and dark molasses (or honey) to the bread maker pan. Stir to dissolve the molasses (or honey).
2. Sprinkle the yeast over the water-molasses mixture in the bread maker pan. Let it sit for 5-10 minutes until frothy.
3. Add the buttermilk, vegetable oil, salt, rye flour, and whole wheat flour to the bread maker pan in that order.
4. If using, add the caraway seeds to the flour.
5. Select the Whole Wheat Bread setting on the bread maker.
6. Start the bread maker. The process of mixing the ingredients will begin.
7. Allow the bread maker to run through its cycle, which typically takes about 3 hours.
8. Once the baking cycle is complete, remove it from the bread maker and place it on a wire rack to cool.
9. Once cooled, slice the Estonian bread (Leib) and serve.

NUTRITION PER SERVING (1 SLICE): CALORIES 140; FAT 3G; CARBS 25G; PROTEIN 3G; FIBER 2G; SODIUM 200MG

MUSTARD BREAD

PREP TIME: 10 MINUTES
RISING TIME: 1-2 HOURS
BAKING TIME: APPROXIMATELY 1 HOUR
COMPLEXITY: BEGINNER

TOOL FUNCTION:
BREAD MAKER OPERATING SETTING: BASIC/WHITE BREAD SETTING BAKING
TEMPERATURE: 375°F (190°C)

TOOLS NEEDED:
BREAD MAKER MEASURING CUPS AND SPOONS MIXING BOWL

INGREDIENTS	1 POUND	1.5 POUND	2 POUND
BREAD FLOUR	1 cup (120 g)	1.5 cups (180 g)	2 cups (240 g)
WHOLE WHEAT FLOUR	1 cup (120 g)	1.5 cups (180 g)	2 cups (240 g)
GRANULATED SUGAR	1 tbsp. (15 g)	1.5 tbsps. (22.5 g)	2 tbsps. (30 g)
SALT	1 tsp. (5 g)	1.5 tsps. (7.5 g)	2 tsps. (10 g)
ACTIVE DRY YEAST	1 tbsp. (15 g)	1.5 tbsps. (22.5 g)	2 tbsps. (30 g)
WARM WATER	¼ cup (60 ml)	⅜ cup (90 ml)	½ cup (120 ml)
MILK	¼ cup (60 ml)	⅜ cup (90 ml)	½ cup (120 ml)
DIJON MUSTARD	1 tbsp. (15 g)	1.5 tbsps. (22.5 g)	2 tbsps. (30 g)
UNSALTED BUTTER	2 tbsps. (30 g)	3 tbsps. (45 g)	4 tbsps. (60 g)
HONEY	1 tbsp. (15 g)	1.5 tbsps. (22.5 g)	2 tbsps. (30 g)

INSTRUCTIONS

1. Add the warm water, sugar, and yeast to the bread maker pan. Stir to dissolve the sugar and yeast. Let it sit for 5-10 minutes until frothy.
2. Add the milk, Dijon mustard, softened butter, honey, salt, bread flour, and whole wheat flour to the pan of the bread maker in the sequence that is listed.
3. Select the Basic/White Bread setting on the bread maker.
4. Start the bread maker. The process of mixing the ingredients will begin.
5. Allow the bread maker to run through its cycle, which typically takes about 3 hours.
6. Once the baking cycle is complete, remove it from the bread maker and place it on a wire rack to cool.
7. Once cooled, slice the mustard bread and serve.

NUTRITION PER SERVING (1 SLICE): CALORIES 120; FAT 2G; CARBS 25G; PROTEIN 2G; FIBER 2G; SODIUM 200MG

TIGER BREAD

PREP TIME: 10 MINUTES
RISING TIME: 1-2 HOURS
BAKING TIME: APPROXIMATELY 1 HOUR
COMPLEXITY: BEGINNER

TOOL FUNCTION:
BREAD MAKER OPERATING SETTING:
BASIC/ WHITE BREAD SETTING BAKING
TEMPERATURE: 375°F (190°C)

TOOLS NEEDED:
BREAD MAKER
MEASURING CUPS AND
SPOONS
MIXING BOWL

INGREDIENTS	1 POUND	1.5 POUND	2 POUND
BREAD FLOUR	1 cup (120 g)	1.5 cups (180 g)	2 cups (240 g)
GRANULATED SUGAR	1 tbsp. (15 g)	1.5 tbsps. (22.5 g)	2 tbsps. (30 g)
SALT	1 tsp. (5 g)	1.5 tsps. (7.5 g)	2 tsps. (10 g)
ACTIVE DRY YEAST	1 tbsp. (15 g)	1.5 tbsps. (22.5 g)	2 tbsps. (30 g)
WARM WATER	¼ cup (60 ml)	⅜ cup (90 ml)	½ cup (120 ml)
VEGETABLE OIL	1 tbsp. (15 ml)	1.5 tbsps. (22.5 ml)	2 tbsps. (30 ml)
RICE FLOUR (TIGER EFFECT)	2 tbsps. (30 g)	3 tbsps. (45 g)	4 tbsps. (60 g)
GRANULATED SUGAR (TIGER EFFECT)	1 tbsp. (15 g)	1.5 tbsps. (22.5 g)	2 tbsps. (30 g)
WARM WATER (TIGER EFFECT)	1 tbsp. (15 ml)	1.5 tbsps. (22.5 ml)	2 tbsps. (30 ml)
SESAME OIL (TIGER EFFECT)	1 tsp. (5 ml)	1.5 tsps. (7.5 ml)	2 tsps. (10 ml)

INSTRUCTIONS

1. Add warm water, sugar, and yeast to the bread maker pan. Stir to dissolve the sugar and yeast. Let it sit for 5-10 minutes until frothy.
2. Add the vegetable oil, salt, and bread flour to the bread maker pan.
3. Select the Basic/White Bread setting on the bread maker.
4. Start the bread maker. The process of mixing the ingredients will begin.
5. While the bread is mixing, prepare the tiger effect mixture. The rice flour, sugar, warm water, and sesame oil should be mixed in a small bowl until forms a thick paste.
6. Once the bread maker has finished kneading and the dough starts to rise, carefully spread the tiger effect paste over the top of the dough, covering it evenly.
7. Ensure that the bread maker's lid is close, and then allow it to continue its cycle.
8. Once the baking cycle is complete, remove it from the bread maker and place it on a wire rack to cool.
9. Once cooled, slice the Tiger Bread and serve.

NUTRITION PER SERVING (1 SLICE): CALORIES 80; FAT 2G; CARBS 14G; PROTEIN 2G; FIBER G; SODIUM 150MG

FINNISH RYE BREAD (RUISLEIPÄ)

PREP TIME: 10 MINUTES
RISING TIME: 1-2 HOURS
BAKING TIME: APPROXIMATELY 1 HOUR
COMPLEXITY: BEGINNER

TOOL FUNCTION:
BREAD MAKER OPERATING SETTING:
WHOLE WHEAT BREAD SETTING
BAKING TEMPERATURE: 375°F (190°C)

TOOLS NEEDED:
BREAD MAKER
MEASURING CUPS AND
SPOONS

INGREDIENTS	1 POUND	1.5 POUND	2 POUND
RYE FLOUR	1 cup (120 g)	1.5 cups (180 g)	2 cups (240 g)
BREAD FLOUR	1 cup (120 g)	1.5 cups (180 g)	2 cups (240 g)
DARK MOLASSES	1 tbsp. (15 g)	1.5 tbsps. (22.5 g)	2 tbsps. (30 g)
SALT	1 tsp. (5 g)	1.5 tsps. (7.5 g)	2 tsps. (10 g)
ACTIVE DRY YEAST	1 tbsp. (15 g)	1.5 tbsps. (22.5 g)	2 tbsps. (30 g)
WARM WATER	½ cup (120 ml)	¾ cup (180 ml)	1 cup (240 ml)
BUTTERMILK	½ cup (120 ml)	¾ cup (180 ml)	1 cup (240 ml)
UNSALTED BUTTER	1 tbsp. (15 g)	1.5 tbsps. (22.5 g)	2 tbsps. (30 g)

INSTRUCTIONS

1. Add warm water and dark molasses to the bread maker pan. Stir to dissolve the molasses.
2. Sprinkle the yeast over the water-molasses mixture in the bread maker pan. Let it sit for 5-10 minutes until frothy.
3. Add the buttermilk, softened butter, salt, rye flour, and bread flour to the bread maker pan in that order.
4. Select the Whole Wheat Bread setting on the bread maker.
5. Start the bread maker. The process of mixing the ingredients will begin.
6. Allow the bread maker to run through its cycle, which typically takes about 3 hours.
7. Once the baking cycle is complete, remove it from the bread maker and place it on a wire rack to cool.
8. Once cooled, slice the Finnish rye bread (Ruisleipä) and serve.

NUTRITION PER SERVING (1 SLICE): CALORIES 140; FAT 2G; CARBS 27G; PROTEIN 2G; FIBER 2G; SODIUM 200MG

FRENCH BREAD WITH MILK POWDER

PREP TIME: 10 MINUTES
RISING TIME: 1-2 HOURS
BAKING TIME: APPROXIMATELY 1 HOUR
COMPLEXITY: BEGINNER

TOOL FUNCTION:
BREAD MAKER OPERATING
SETTING: BASIC/ WHITE BREAD
SETTING BAKING TEMPERATURE:
375°F (190°C)

TOOLS NEEDED:
BREAD MAKER MEASURING CUPS
AND SPOONS MIXING BOWL

INGREDIENTS	1 POUND	1.5 POUND	2 POUND
BREAD FLOUR	1 cup (120 g)	1.5 cups (180 g)	2 cups (240 g)
MILK POWDER	1 tbsp. (8 g)	1.5 tbsps. (12 g)	2 tbsps. (16 g)
SUGAR	1 tsp. (5 g)	1.5 tsps. (7 g)	2 tsps. (10 g)
SALT	½ tsp. (3 g)	¾ tsp. (4.5 g)	1 tsp. (6 g)
UNSALTED BUTTER	1 tbsp. (15 g)	1.5 tbsps. (22 g)	2 tbsps. (30 g)
ACTIVE DRY YEAST	1 tsp. (5 g)	1.5 tsps. (7.5 g)	2 tsps. (10 g)
WARM WATER	⅓ cup (80 ml)	½ cup (120 ml)	⅔ cup (160 ml)
MILK	1 tbsp. (15 ml)	1.5 tbsps. (22.5 ml)	2 tbsps. (30 ml)

INSTRUCTIONS

1. Sugar and warm water should be added to the bread maker pan. Stir to dissolve the sugar.
2. Sprinkle the yeast over the water-sugar mixture in the bread maker pan. Let it sit for 5-10 minutes until frothy.
3. Add the softened butter, salt, bread flour, and milk powder to the bread maker pan in that order.
4. Select the Basic or White Bread setting setting on the bread maker.
5. Start the bread maker. The process of mixing the ingredients will begin.
6. Allow the bread maker to run through its cycle, which typically takes about 3 hours.
7. Once the baking cycle is complete, remove it from the bread maker and place it on a wire rack to cool.
8. Once cooled, slice the French bread with milk powder and serve.

NUTRITION PER SERVING (1 SLICE): CALORIES 120; FAT 2G; CARBS 24G; PROTEIN 2G; FIBER 2G; SODIUM 200MG

INDEX

Made in the USA
Columbia, SC
08 June 2025

59001016R00043